Junkers
Ju 288/388/488

Karl-Heinz Regnat

MIDLAND
An imprint of
Ian Allan Publishing

Junkers Ju 288/388/488
© Bernard & Graefe Verlag, 2002, 2004

ISBN 1 85780 173 3

First published 2002 in Germany by
Bernard & Graefe Verlag, Bonn

Translation from original German text
by Ted Oliver

English language edition published 2004 by
Midland Publishing
4 Watling Drive, Hinckley, LE10 3EY, England
Tel: 01455 254 490   Fax: 01455 254 495
E-mail: midlandbooks@compuserve.com

Midland Publishing is an imprint of
Ian Allan Publishing Ltd

Worldwide distribution (except North America):
Midland Counties Publications
4 Watling Drive, Hinckley, LE10 3EY, England
Telephone: 01455 254 450   Fax: 01455 233 737
E-mail: midlandbooks@compuserve.com
www.midlandcountiessuperstore.com

North American trade distribution:
Specialty Press Publishers & Wholesalers Inc.
39966 Grand Avenue, North Branch, MN 55056
Tel: 651 277 1400   Fax: 651 277 1203
Toll free telephone: 800 895 4585
www.specialtypress.com

Design concept and layout
© 2004 Midland Publishing and
Stephen Thompson Associates

Printed in England by
Ian Allan Printing Ltd
Riverdene Business Park, Molesey Road,
Hersham, Surrey, KT12 4RG

Title page illustration:
**The Ju 388 V3 (PG+YB) prototype of the
bomber variant, powered by BMW 801J radials.**

Contents

Chapters

Chapter One

Bomber Designs

Favoured and then Discarded

The 'Bomber B' Programme

The motivation for the RLM *Technisches Amt* (Technical Office) to initiate this manufacturing programme in July 1939 was, on the one hand, the search for a suitable successor to the 'workhorse' Ju 88A and its Heinkel He 111 counterpart, and on the other, to fill the gap in the tactical area between the Ju 88 and the He 177 'Bomber A'. The underlying idea was to create a new generation consisting of a multi-purpose bomber and a fast bomber. Until then, the preferred solution had been the fast-, medium- and heavy-bomber. Much was expected of the 'Bomber B', but for a variety of reasons it became a bitter disappointment. The Ju 288 or Fw 191 would at the very least have significantly increased the fighting power of the Luftwaffe, if it had not been for the problems associated with their hydraulic and electrical systems. In mid-1939, the specification was issued to both Junkers and Focke-Wulf. At the end of that year, Ju 88 production was still in its initial phase and a mere 69 examples had left the assembly lines. By this time, Arado, Dornier and Henschel had also been drawn into the 'Bomber B' project. The designers had to take the following requirements into account:

- layout as a twin-engined aircraft
- provision of a pressurised cabin
- a crew of three
- remote-controlled weapon stations
- use of the DB 604 or Jumo 222 motors
- a maximum speed of 670km/h (416mph)
- ability to carry a bombload of up to 2,000kg (4,409 lb) at 600km/h at 7,000m (373mph at 22,965ft) to a target 1,800km (1,118 miles) away.

Junkers had an advantage over its competitors because as early as 1937 it had worked on the EF 73 design proposal. This *Entwicklungs-Flugzeug* (Development Aircraft) consisted of a twin-engined high-altitude bomber powered by the Jumo 222 or Jumo 223. The EF 73 had already been submitted to the RLM in November 1937 and was to serve as a valuable foundation for the later development of the Ju 288.

As mentioned above, five firms altogether took part in this competition, the most favoured aircraft undoubtedly being the Ju 288 and the Fw 191. The latter was technically an extremely interesting aircraft, but the considerable expenditure on its technical refinements was to result in it suffering the same fate as the Ar 340, Do 317 and the Hs 130C.

The Competitors

Arado Ar 340

In terms of wing dimensions and loaded weight, the Ar 340 corresponded roughly to those of its counterparts but it differed considerably in its overall configuration, its origins having stemmed from the Ar E 500 project of 1936. The design featured a central fuselage nacelle, twin booms and a trapezoidal wing, and it was powered by the Jumo 222 or DB 604.

The fuselage was of circular cross-section with a pressurised cabin for a crew of three, and had dorsal and ventral remote-controlled weapon positions. An additional machine-gun was housed at its rear extremity as well as at the ends of the tapering tailbooms. Defensive armament of the Ar 340 therefore consisted of two paired and three single turrets equipped with MG 131s or MG 151s, periscopic sights being employed for target sighting. As far as the turrets were concerned, Arado undertook development work in collaboration not only with the Askania, Goertz and Siemens firms but also with the DVL aeronautical research institute.

A wind-tunnel model of the Junkers EF 73 proposal.

The Arado Ar 340 contribution to the 'Bomber B' programme. An unconventional solution, it was unsuccessful.

The offensive load of a maximum of 6,000kg (13,228lb) of bombs of various types was to have been completely enclosed internally in the bomb bay. Unlike the Focke-Wulf Fw189, Fokker G.1, Lockheed P-38 Lightning and the Lockheed XP-58 Chain Lightning, where the tailbooms were joined by a central tailplane, the Ar340 featured tailplane halves mounted on the twin fins and rudders on the outboard portions only, as seen in the illustration. Overall length of the aircraft was 18.65m (61ft 2¼in).

The trapezoidal wing of 23m (75ft 5½in) span and 69m² (742.69ft²) area housed the fuel tanks. Equipped weight was 11,680kg (25,750lb) and take-off weight 17,800kg (39,242lb). With a 2,000kg (4,409lb) bombload, a theoretical range of 3,600km (2,237 miles) was possible. Up to this point, the data for both E340 variants was identical. In terms of ceiling, however, the Jumo 222 and DB604 variants stood in the ratio of 8,900m (29,200ft) to 9,700m (31,825ft), but in maximum and cruising speeds they could attain 630km/h (391mph) and 473km/h (294mph) respectively.

A mock-up built by Arado in 1940 was evaluated by RLM personnel at the end of the year and was found on the whole to be satisfactory except for the bomb-release system which gave grounds for criticism. Following revisions, the design was resubmitted to the RLM *Technisches Amt* on 28th February 1941, only for the E340 to be rejected outright. This was a considerable slap in the face, as Arado had firmly counted on an order for ten test prototypes.

Dornier Do 317

Unlike Arado, where, faced with a new situation, recourse was made to the construction of a mock-up, Dornier was able to advance its development to at least prototype status. In all, six V-models had been ordered, the Do 317 V1 (VK+IY) having made its maiden flight on 8th September 1943 – exceedingly late, since the Ju 288 V1 had already undertaken its first flight on 29th November 1940. At first glance, the new Do 317 was very similar to its Do 217 forebear. On closer inspection, however, considerable changes were apparent, particularly in the provision of a pressurised cabin (as required by the specification) with which Dornier had already gained experience on the Do 217PV-1, but which would ultimately come to fruition with the Do 317B. With this design, Dornier had evolved two versions: the Do 317A represented by the Do 317 V1, and the Do 317B prototype whose components only partly existed.

The airframe dimensions of the Do 317 V1 differed from those of the Do 217, its fuselage having a greater capacity by reason of its enlarged cross-section. The ability to be able to carry a heavier bombload was perhaps only one of the reasons. Particularly noticeable was the drastic alteration made to the vertical tail surfaces where, instead of the usual trapezoidal plan form, an unusual pointed triangular shape was chosen. As on the later Do 217 models, powerplant was the DB603. Despite the overall similarity of both Dornier designs, only a few parts of the Do 217 could be used in the Do 317. Defensive armament of the Do 317A (the V1 prototype was unarmed) consisted of:

- 1 x MG 131 in an electrically operated dorsal fuselage turret
- 1 x MG 151 in a fixed installation
- 1 x MG 81Z in the fuselage nose, and
- 2 x MG 131s directed rearwards in the upper and lower crew area.

Flight trials with the Do 317 V1 began on 9th September 1943, but it failed to live up to expectations. Performance was no better than that of the Do 217P-0, so the engineers were required to make further improvements.

The real object of the 'Bomber B' programme had been the Do 317B, which was to incorporate the required full-view pressurised cabin for the crew of four. In order to achieve improved performance at high altitudes, the wingspan was increased from the original 20.64m (67ft 8⅝in) on the Do 317A to 26m (85ft 3⅝in) on the Do 317B. On the powerplant side, the DB 610 was decided upon. As opposed to the Do 317A, defensive armament was to have been concentrated in four remote-controlled positions, namely:

- a B1-Stand (2 x MG 131) behind the cockpit
- a B2-Stand (2 x MG 131) roughly at the fuselage centre
- a C-Stand (1 x MG 81Z) beneath the cockpit, and
- an H-Stand (1 x MG 151) in the fuselage tail.

In accordance with requirements, the offensive load consisted of a 4,000kg (8,818lb) bomb-load. Performance calculations gave a maximum speed of 585km/h at 6,000m (364mph at 19,685ft) rated altitude when powered by the Jumo 222. The Do 317A reached a maximum of 560km/h (348mph) at this altitude. With two DB 610A/B engines, the Do 317B was theoretically capable of attaining an impressive maximum speed of 770km/h at 11,340m (478mph at 37,200ft). Maximum take-off weight of the Do 317A was 18,650kg (41,116lb) with

Frontal view of the Do 317 V1. Its development from the Do 217 is readily apparent.

In contrast to the Ju 288, a whole series of functions on the Fw 191 were to have been operated via servo-motors.

the DB 603 and 20,150kg (44,423 lb) with the Jumo 222, the maximum weight for the Do 317B being almost 4,000kg (8,818 lb) more, at 24,000kg (52,910 lb).

Even with the Do 317B project, dark clouds appeared over the horizon. In common with similar prototypes, problems involving the high-altitude engines, as well as events surrounding the Ju 188, led to further development being aborted. Only the Do 317 V1 remained from the Do 317B programme, together with parts of the other machines only partially built, was consigned to the scrapheap. This fate, however, was not shared by the five remaining Do 317A test prototypes. These exotic mach-ines were specially modified for attacks on shipping, and as the Do 217R, were integrated into the Luftwaffe's aircraft inventory. These guided-bomb carriers saw operational service with III/KG 100.

Focke-Wulf Fw 191

The Fw 191 developed from the end of 1939 under the leadership of Dipl.-Ing. Rudiger Kosel. In the final phase it was the runner-up to the favoured Ju 288 in the 'Bomber B' competition. But it was also affected by the engine problems that dogged the entire 'Bomber B' project. Owing to the lack of the urgently needed Jumo 222, the BMW 801 had to be used as a stopgap. The engine competing with the Jumo 222, the DB 604, had meanwhile been deleted from the development list. As the Jumo 222 would certainly never attain series production maturity, recourse had to be made to the DB 603 or DB 610 in order to keep the project alive at all. Faced with this situation, Focke-Wulf considered other options, among them a four-engined variant powered by the Jumo 211 and designated Fw 191C (Fw 491). This scheme met with a sympathetic response from those responsible in the RLM.

The Fw 191 V1 prototype made its maiden flight at the beginning of 1942. A short while later it was followed in trials by the second prototype, both machines being powered by BMW 801 radials.

The all-metal monocoque-construction fuselage of oval cross-section retained this form right up to the convergent tail section, the overall length of all variants remaining constant at 18.45m (60ft 6⅜in). The four-man crew cabin formed a pressurised compartment with braced clear-vision panels. A trapezoidal tailplane combined with almost rectangular endplate fins and rudders completed the structure at the rear of the fuselage. The mid-positioned wing centre section housing the powerplants and rearward-retracting main undercarriage units was attached to the trapezoidal outer wing sections.

For the Fw 191A, span was 25m (82ft 0¼in) and wing area 70.5m² (758.84ft²); for the Fw 191B and C, span and area were increased to 26m (85ft 3⅜in) and 75m² (807.27ft²) respectively. The problem of fulfilling the required performance specifications was compounded by the unavailability of the originally intended powerplants. Besides the Fw 191A powered by the DB 603, there was the Fw 191B powered by coupled DB 610 engines. The previously mentioned Fw 191C was designed as a four-engined aircraft with the Jumo 211, but this was an unwise decision, since four separate engines caused an appreciable increase in drag. The individual variants had the following powerplants at their disposal:

- Jumo 222: 2 x 2,000hp = 4,000hp
- DB 603: 2 x 1,750hp = 3,500hp
- DB 610: 2 x 2,950hp = 5,900hp
- Jumo 211: 4 x 1,420hp = 5,680hp
- BMW 801: 2 x 1,800hp = 3,600hp.

The 6,000 litre (1,320 gal) fuel capacity of the Fw 191A was housed in five protected SG bag-tanks above the bomb bay, each capable of holding 960 litres, plus two tanks in the wing centre section. As required by the specification, the Fw 191A could carry a 4,000kg (8,818 lb) bombload and, if desired, could also accommodate 2 x LT 950 torpedoes in the bomb bay as well as two more as external loads.

The description of the aircraft so far is strictly conventional – apart from the pressurised cabin and the remote-controlled armament positions. However, the novelty with the Fw 191 lay in its ability to carry out all the normal hydraulically or mechanically operated functions by electrical means. The impetus for this came from the RLM. This was done in order to establish whether the Junkers hydraulically operated systems, employed for every conceivable function in the Ju 288, would turn out to be the more suitable method in the Fw 191, armed with a whole series of electro-motors supporting its technology. But already during the initial trials phase the design philosophy based on servo-motors had proved susceptible to breakdowns. For example, various defects became apparent where the electrically operated systems effected control commands for flap operation either erroneously or not at all. Trials with the first two prototypes were abruptly ended after only 10 hours, and Focke-Wulf was far from happy with the RLM's insistence that as many functions as possible be carried out electrically. Whilst such innovations might have proved useful in a civil aircraft, in a military machine this solution was more than questionable. From the high maintenance aspect alone, the personnel at frontline airfields were confronted with several problems which they would not otherwise have had to face. The susceptibility to enemy fire and resultant damage that was a constant factor to be contended with in an operational aircraft would have led to a drastic increase in maintenance effort. As the war progressed, support personnel in frontline squadrons would be withdrawn for other duties, thereby creating an even more extensive problem.

The Fw 191, although technically advanced, had to contend with weight problems, not the least of which were the many kilometres of necessary cables. As a result of unsatisfactory performance, the RLM ordered the cancellation of the Fw 191 V3 to V5 prototypes in rapid succession. Soon afterwards, however, two of the all-too-rare Jumo 222 motors were assigned to the firm. In addition, Dipl.-Ing. Kosel received RLM approval to replace the troublesome portions of the electrical systems with hydraulic components. The tide had at least turned for a short while. The sixth prototype, equipped with

The Ju 288 mock-up of how the aircraft was later to appear.

Jumo 222A/B engines, was completed and flight trials began. Unlike its predecessors, this prototype had various hydraulically operated systems, including the undercarriage, and instead of the so-called 'Multhopp flaps' (four-part combined dive and landing flaps) conventional flaps were installed. The initial flight of the Fw 191 V6 took place in spring 1943, but subsequent events nullified an extensive series of flight trials as the RLM showed no further interest in the 'Bomber B' programme and, with it, the Fw 191.

Henschel Hs 130C

The Henschel firm was the fourth of the competitors to the Ju 288 and had already gained considerable experience with pressurised cabins – the core of a high-flying fighter, bomber or reconnaissance aircraft. It was here, at the end of 1939, that the first of two Hs 128 prototypes appeared that formed the basis for the Hs 130 high-altitude reconnaissance aircraft. Some ten examples were built but were never used operationally. Originally equipped with the DB 601R, the aircraft were later used as test-beds for the DB 605 or Jumo 208 engines.

The Hs 130B high-altitude bomber version was based on the Hs 130A. A completely different variant was the Hs 130C high-altitude bomber which had a different configuration altogether and represented a new design. Work on this model began in late 1940, the crew of four in this case also being housed in a pressurised cabin. In terms of design, it differed considerably from the Hs 130 service models that had preceded it and was more akin to the Do 317 which, as already stated, featured a full clear-vision canopy divided by metal bracing.

The all-metal monocoque fuselage had an overall length of 18.57m (60ft 11⅛in). In contrast to the low-winged Hs 130A, it had a shoulder-mounted wing of span 24.7m (79ft 0½in) and area 67.48m² (726.33ft²). Whilst the Hs 130C was to have been powered by the BMW 801, the V2 prototype was to have the BMW 801J, and the V3 the DB 603A. It is probable that a variant powered by the Jumo 222 was considered, but there is no documentary evidence to confirm this. More, on the other hand, can be said of the armament proposals for the Hs 130 V3 which was to consist of:

- an A-Stand (2 x MG 131) remote-controlled, beneath the fuselage nose
- a B-Stand (2 x MG 131) remote-controlled, above the pressurised cabin
- an H-Stand (1 x MG 15) in the fuselage tail, and
- a maximum bombload of 4,000kg (8,818 lb).

The sum of all its component parts, installations and payload resulted in a maximum take-off weight of 19,960kg (44,004 lb). Maximum speed, with reduced payload, however, was in the region of 513km/h at 5,100m (319mph at 16,730ft). Calculated values at higher altitudes are unfortunately not available.

From 1941, three Hs 130C prototypes were under construction. How far advanced towards completion they were is unclear. If one is to believe the sources, it appears that at least one prototype equipped with the BMW 801J was completed. Mention should also be made here of the Hs 130D project powered by two DB 616 engines, and the Hs 130E high-altitude bomber of which a prototype flew for the first time in September 1942. Even these versions of the Hs 130, however, never achieved series-production status.

So much for the details of designs competing with the Ju 288 in the course of the ill-fated 'Bomber B' programme that suffered several setbacks and finally perished as a result. The most significant of these was the ever-present motor problem. Technical and design difficulties, coupled with a lack of materials as well as changes in priorities, caused the initially promising programme to fall to pieces.

Technical Data Comparison

	Arado Ar 340	Dornier Do 317B	Focke-Wulf Fw 191A	Focke-Wulf Fw 191B	Henschel Hs 130C	Junkers Ju 288A
Powerplant						
Designation	Jumo 222	DB 610A/B	Jumo 222	DB 610A/B	DB 603A	Jumo 222A/B
Take-off power, hp	2 x 2000	2 x 2870	2 x 2000	2 x 2950	2 x 1750	2 x 2000
Dimensions						
Wingspan	23.00m (75' 5½")	26.00m (85' 3⅝")	25.00m (82' 0¼")	26.00m (85' 3⅝")	24.70m (81' 0½")	22.00m (72' 2.1")
Length	18.65m (61' 2¼")	16.80m (53' 1⅜")	18.45m (60' 6⅜")	18.45m (60' 6⅜")	18.57m (60' 11⅛")	16.60m (54' 5.5")
Height	5.15m (16' 10¾")	5.45m (17' 10½")	4.80m (15' 9")	4.80m (15' 9")	- -	4.60m (15' 1.1")
Wing area, m² (ft²)	69.00 (742.69)	75.00 (807.27)	70.50 (758.84)	75.00 (807.27)	67.48 (726.33)	60.00 (645.82)
Weights						
Equipped weight, kg (lb)	11,680 (25,750)	- -	11,465 (25,276)	16,500 (36,376)	- -	11,000 (24,251)
Fuel weight, kg (lb)	- -	- -	4,390 (9,678)	4,390 (9,678)	- -	3,300 (7,275)
Lubricant weight, kg (lb)	- -	- -	350 772	500 1,102	- -	300 661
Take-off weight max, kg (lb)	17,800 (39,242)	24,000 (2,910)	19,575 (43,155)	23,800 (52,469)	19,960 (44,004)	17,300 (38,140)
Wing loading, kg/m² (lbft²)	258 (52.84)	320 (65.50)	278 (56.87)	317 (65.00)	266 (60.58)	288 (59.06)
Performance						
Maximum speed	580km/h at 6,000m (360mph at 19,685ft)	669km/h at 7,620m (416mph at 25,000m)	620km/h at 6,350m (385mph at 20,835)	635km/h at 6,350m (395mph at 20,835ft)	513km/h at 5,100m (319mph at 16,730ft)	645km/h at 6,000m (401mph at 19,685ft)
Cruising speed	473km/h at 8,000m (294mph at 26,250ft)	539km/h at 6,000m (335mph at 19,685ft)	550km/h at 6,000m (342mph at 19,685ft)	550km/h at 6,000m (342mph at 19,685ft)	- -	565km/h at 6,000m (351mph at 19,685ft)
Range max, km (miles)	3,600 (2,237)	4,000 (2,486)	3,600 (2,237)	3,050 (1,895)	3,330 (2,069)	3,850 (2,392)
Service Ceiling, m (ft)	8,900 (29,200)	10,520 (34,515)	9,700 (31,825)	8,800 (28,870)	7,925 (26,000)	10,300 (33,790)
Military Load						
Bombload						
Internal, kg (lb)	4,000 (8,818)	5,600 (12,346)	2,120 (4,674)	2,000 (4,409)	4,000 (8,818)	3,000 (6,514)
External, kg, (lb)	- -	3,600 (7,937)	none -	1,000 (2,205)	- -	2,000 (4,409)
Armament	2 x DL = 2 x MG 131 or 2 x MG 151					
- A-Stand	-	-	1 x MG 81Z	1 x MG 151	1 x MG 131r/c	(deleted)
- B-Stand	-	-	1 x FDL 151/81	1 x FDL 151/81	2 x MG 131r/c	2 x MG 131r/c
- B1-Stand	-	2 x MG 131	-	-	-	-
- B2-Stand	-	2 x MG131FT	-	-	-	-
- C-Stand	-	2 x MG 81KT	1x FDL 151/81	1 x FDL MG 131	2 x MG 131	2 x MG 131r/c
- D-Stand	-	-	2 x MG 81Z	(deleted)	-	-
- H-Stand	3 x MG 131or 3 x MG 151r/c	FHL with 1 x MG 151/20	- -	1 x MG 151 or 2 x MG 131	1 x MG 15 -	- -
Crew	Four	Four	Four	Four	Four	Three

DL = Drehlafette (rotatable turret); FDL = Ferngesteuerte DL (remote-controlled DL); FT = Ferngesteuerte Turm (r/c turret); KT = Kinnturm (chin turret); FHL = Fernhecklafette (remote-controlled tail turret); r/c = remote-controlled

Chapter Two

The Ju 288 V1 to V108 Prototypes

As mentioned in Chapter 1, two designs emerged as front-runners from the 'Bomber B' specification. The Fw 191 followed a different technical approach from the Ju 288 bomber design developed under the leadership of Professor Dr.-Ing. Heinrich Hertel. Extensive efforts in terms of planning and design bore fruit in the Ju 288 V1. Professor Hertel had anticipated that the V1 would be ready to fly in October 1940, with series production planned for the beginning of 1942, but these deadlines proved impossible to meet. His Chief Designer, Dipl.-Ing Ernst Zindel, with his greater insight into the complexity of engine manufacture, knew of the prevailing difficulties associated with the powerplant and was therefore less enthusiastic. It was clear to him that Professor Hertel's proposed timescale was far too optimistic. Unfortunately, events proved Zindel right as the catastrophe with the Jumo 222 clearly showed, and resulted in the first four prototypes being powered by the obligatory BMW 801G.

Before the construction phase at Junkers could begin, however, there were several other hurdles to be overcome. The Ju 288 mock-up was inspected by representatives of the RLM *Technisches Amt* (Technical Office) towards the end of November 1939 and was judged favourably, giving Junkers the green light to proceed with further work. In May 1940, the complete fuselage mock-up was evaluated by the RLM, resulting in an order for three proto-types. In anticipation of this decision, Professor Hertel had as early as December 1939 issued instructions for parts manufacture of the Ju 288 V1 to begin. The Ju 88 V2 (D-AREN) and the Ju 88 V5 (D-ATYU) had previously been modified to incorporate the forward fuselage section of the Ju 288 so that initial handling experience could be obtained in flight. The data gathered during test flights since the summer of 1940 by *Flugkapitäne* Siegfried Holzbauer, Werner Joop and Reinhold Preuschen were generally encouraging. During this phase, two different types of dive-brakes were tested, since the Ju 288 was also to have dive-bombing capability. In the autumn of 1940, strength tests were carried out on the Ju 288 static test airframe.

Following the completion of numerous ground tests, the moment of truth for everyone involved on the project finally arrived – somewhat belatedly – on 29th November 1940, when the Ju 288 V1 stood ready for its maiden flight. It was now time for the hard reality of flight trials to confirm the great expectations that had been placed in the aircraft. From the performance aspect, however, the Ju 288 V1 failed to live up to aspirations due to its lower-powered BMW 801 engines. The difference in power with that of the Jumo 222 was too great. It was only on 8th October 1941 that a giant leap forward was finally made when the Ju 288 V5, equipped with the more powerful units, took off on its maiden flight. Its improved performance was especially noticeable at high altitudes where the power of the BMW 801 decreased from 1,600hp at take-off to 1,380hp.

We shall now examine the events concerning the numerous Ju 288 prototypes, grouped under related headings according to their respective powerplants.

Publisher's Note: Principal data and installation features that applied to or were common to individual prototypes are provided in a Prototype Data Table, so that only the significant differences between them are related below.

BMW 801-Powered Ju 288 Initial Prototypes

Ju 288 V1

This prototype, *Werknummer* (construction number) 2880001, was the first of this sequentially numbered series of prototypes. With the civil registration D-AACS (other sources erroneously mention D-AOTF),* it made its first flight on 29th November 1940. It was equipped, as were all subsequent prototypes, with a pressurised cockpit for a crew of three, but had only a short

Port view of the BMW 801-powered Ju 288 V1 in its factory-finished state before livery was applied. First flight was on 29th November 1940.

Top left: **This view accentuates the slim rectangular fuselage and the steel-braced pressurised cabin for the crew of three.**

Top right: **Behind the Ju 288 V1 is the Ju 88 V15.**

Above: **A frontal view of the Ju 288 V1 with raised rear fuselage.**

Right: **The Ju 288 V1 is seen here in Luftwaffe colours RLM 70/71/65 and civil registration D-AACS.**

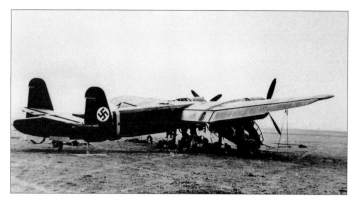

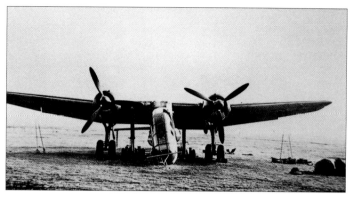

Top left, top right and centre left: **Three views of the extensive damage suffered by the Ju 288 V1 in the emergency landing following the port engine fire in flight. The endplate fins and rudders sported a red band with the black swastika enclosed in a white disc. The letters D-AACS are hardly visible on the fuselage sides.**

Centre right: **The result of the engine fire is visible above the port wing, as is the displaced alignment of the flying surfaces.**

Left: **The fire had so weakened the structure that the entire crew compartment collapsed at the junction with the wing root leading-edge.**

flying life as it suffered extensive structural damage as the result of an engine fire during its test flight on 2nd March 1941 and had to be written off after the emergency landing. The B-Stand and C-Stand dorsal and ventral fuselage armament positions on this machine were installed as mock-ups. Powerplants, dimensions and other salient details are listed in the accompanying Prototype Data Table (q.v.).

*Photographs of the Ju 288 V1 clearly show the letters D-AACS on both upper and lower wing surfaces. The often-quoted D-AOTF seems to have originated as a corruption of D-ACTF on the Ju 288 V3.

Ju 288 V2

This machine, c/n 2880002, civil registration D-ABWP, made its first flight on 1st March 1941. During the course of flight trials, it received the military call-sign BG+GR. The undercarriage was damaged in landing accidents in January and July 1942, but whether the prototype was repaired after the second incident is not known. Like its predecessor, the B-Stand and C-Stand armament positions on the V2 were mock-ups. On the V2, which featured an increased wingspan and a nose-mounted instrument probe,

lattice-type dive-brakes were fitted on the upper and lower surfaces of the outboard landing flaps.

Ju 288 V3

The first flight of the V3 (D-ACTP) was on 18th April 1941. Initially test-flown in Rechlin at the end of April as BG+GS, flight trials continued until June 1941. With this prototype, too, the first accidents were not long in coming, again caused by undercarriage weakness. Although strengthened when repaired after the first such incident, the results were still regarded as unsatisfactory, so the Ju 88 V16 (D-ACAR) was called on to take part in undercarriage trials. The flight-cleared V3 was later modified, but suffered damage once more in a landing accident. Shortly before this it had successfully accomplished its 100th flight.

The V3 prototype, initially fitted with mock-up B-, C2- and H-Stand weapon positions, was also tested in Tarnewitz with various armament installations including the FA-15 tail barbette. Although overall length and height remained unchanged, wingspan was further increased to 22m (72ft 2in).

Ju 288 V4

The V4, initially D-ADVR and later BG+GT, was the last of the prototypes powered by BMW 801G radials driving three-bladed VDM airscrews and flew for the first time on 17th May 1941. Shortly after its initial flight, the testing phase came to an abrupt end when the port engine caught fire during a landing approach. As a result of severe damage to the weakened fuselage structure, the fuselage nose collapsed during the landing run. The prototype, however, was able to be repaired, but damage removal lasted until November 1941. The crew in this case escaped unharmed.

With the V4, the mock-up B- and C-Stands of the earlier prototypes were replaced by actual weapon installations, but the dive-brakes were discarded. On this aircraft, wingspan was 20.2m (66ft 3¼in) as on the Ju 288 V2.

Ju 288 V7

This prototype rolled out after final assembly in June 1942, entering military trials as BG+GW, and made its maiden flight in July 1942. Beginning on 6th August, extensive diving trials were conducted up to diving speeds of 670km/h

Above and right: **The Ju 288 V2 (D-ABWP), seen here with its nose measurement probe, is accompanied by the Ju 88 V16 (D-ACAR) at right. First flight was on 1st March 1941.**

Below: **Unlike the first prototype, the civil registration is clearly visible in this view of the Ju 288 V2.**

Bottom pair: **The Ju 288 V2 on 20th July 1942 following the partial collapse of its starboard undercarriage that revealed its inherent weakness.**

(416mph). Technically, it corresponded to the V6 prototype except for the BMW 801C engines installed due to the scarcity of the Jumo 222. The V7 was fitted with a new tail section corresponding to that intended for the Ju 288B version, but with only mock-ups in its B-, C-, and H-Stand weapon stations. In the course of flight trials, it also suffered structural damage when the starboard engine caught fire and collapsed, but with little other visible damage. Overall dimensions were increased on all three axes and reflected those of the Ju 288B.

Ju 288 V10

The exact date when flight trials began with this prototype (DF+CP) cannot be established, but it was presumably in the summer of 1942.

Opposite page:

Top left: **The Ju 288 V3, first flown on 18th April 1941, is seen here without the nose measurement probe.**

Top right: **Although unfortunately not an original photograph, this impression of the V3 nevertheless provides useful external details for the modeller.**

Centre: **The V3 was also completed in RLM colours 70/71/65, but with the endplate swastika in its white disc moved further aft over the rudder.**

Bottom: **A group photograph taken after the 100th flight of the Ju 288 V3.**

Photographs on this page:

Top left: **The BMW 801C-powered Ju 288 V7 seen after the starboard engine collapsed following fire damage that weakened the nacelle attachment structure.**

Top right: **In this view, the wool tufts clearly visible on the port wing are to study the airflow patterns on the V7, equipped with the Ju 288B tail assembly.**

This view emphasises the ducted radiator intake for the Jumo 222. In the background is the Ju 288 V3 (D-ACTF).

As opposed to the Jumo 222-powered V8 and V9 prototypes that preceded it, the V10 was equipped with the high-altitude BMW 801TJ fitted with exhaust-gas superchargers to boost altitude performance, although the latter did not exactly meet with the expectations of Junkers and the RLM. Incorporating a four-man pressure cabin and B- and C-Stand mock-ups, the V10 was used for trials with a landing approach altitude. On this prototype, wingspan was 22.6m (74ft 1¾in) as on the Ju 288 V7.

Jumo 222-Powered Ju 288A-Series Prototypes

Ju 288 V5

The Ju 288 V5 (BG+GU), the first of the Ju 288A-series prototypes to be powered by the long-awaited Jumo 222A/B driving four-bladed VS 7 propellers and annular radiator duct, was rolled out after final assembly in July and made its maiden flight on 8th October 1941. Aft of the three-man pressurised cabin, it also had mock-up B- and C-Stand weapons and was dimensionally identical to the short-span V1 prototype.

Ju 288 V6

Initially D-AFDN and later BG+GV, this prototype was the next to be fitted with the Jumo 222A/B powerplants. Since the RLM had in the meantime demanded an increase in pay load, the airframe was also appreciably modified and had new ailerons. Wingspan was increased to 22.6m (74ft 1¾in) and wing area to 64.7m² (696.42ft²). Its maiden flight took place on 18th January 1942, but during the course of trials it had to make an emergency landing due to an engine fire. As a result of the ensuing severe damage the aircraft had to be written off. Armament consisted of an MG 131Z and mock-up C- and H-Stands.

Ju 288 V8

The third Ju 288A-series prototype, the V8 (RD+MU) first flown in April 1942, incorporated the characteristic features of the favoured Ju 288B model which included larger overall dimensions as listed in the data table. Other than having mock-up B- and C-Stand weapon positions, no further details are available on its further development or eventual fate.

Top left: **The Ju 288 V8 under construction. Likewise powered by the Jumo 222, it featured the Ju 288B tail assembly. The first confirmed flight was on 3rd September 1942.**

Top right: **The Ju 288 V12 under construction, with the V13 prototype in the background. First flight took place in June 1942.**

Above right: **The Ju 288 V14, powered by the Jumo 222A/B, presumably made its first flight in September 1942. Finished in the usual RLM colours 70/71/65, the call-sign letters DF+CT are visible here beneath the wings and on the fuselage sides.**

Left three photographs: **This Ju 288 V9, ordered in September 1941, flew for the first time on 2nd May 1942. Finished in RLM colours 70/71/65, it had a pressurised cabin housing a crew of four. Although the underwing code letters VE+QP are clearly visible, these cannot be seen on the fuselage sides.**

Ju 288 V9

The V9, c/n 2880009 (VE+QP), represented the first of the Ju 288B-series prototypes which now had a four-man pressurised crew compartment, together with the enlarged dimensions and new tail assembly. In addition to its mock-up B- and C-Stand weapons, it featured a so-called 'chin' turret equipped with an MG 151/20 cannon. Shortly after its first flight on 2nd May 1942, the aircraft was ferried over to the Rechlin test centre, making its first flight there on 11th May. The Jumo 222A/B engines initially installed were later replaced by the more powerful Jumo 222E/F. In place of the annular tunnel-type intake channels of the V5, the aircraft reverted to normal unducted airscrews.

Ju 288 V12

The V12 (DF+CR), first flown in June 1942, was completed as a hybrid airframe featuring the three-man pressurised cabin of the Ju 288A version combined with the enlarged dimensions and empennage of the Ju 288B. Its B-Stand weapon consisted of an FDL 131Z.

Ju 288 V14

The V14 (DF+CT) was the last of the six Jumo 222A/B-powered prototypes to leave the assembly lines in August 1942, and was also the last in which its c/n number corresponded to the last two digits of this *Werknummer* series. As with the V8, it was fitted with mock-up B- and C-Stand weapon stations. The aircraft is thought to have made its first flight in September 1942.

The subsequent flight-test phase turned out to be so successful that the RLM considered placing a series-production order powered by the 'fall-back' DB 606 engine as an alternative powerplant. Further details of this prototype, however, are currently unknown.

DB 606-Powered Ju 288B-Series Prototypes

Ju 288 V11

The V11 was the first of the Ju 288B-series prototypes powered by the DB 606A/B as a substitute for the scarce Jumo 222A/B. Initially D-ANXN and later DF+CQ, it left the final

Top left: **The Ju 288 V11, rolled out in May 1942, made its first flight in July 1942. Visible here is the widened four-crew pressurised cabin and lateral panels which replaced the side blisters on the BMW 801 and Jumo 222-powered prototypes, and the ventral periscope.**

Top right and above left: **These views clearly show the DB 606 widened engine nacelles and the widened four-man high-altitude pressurised crew compartment of the V11 whilst raised for undercarriage tests.**

Centre right and bottom right: **Two views of the Ju 288 V13 on the occasion of its crash-landing on 16th May 1943 when it ploughed a path through a cornfield. On the lower photograph, the lifting trapeze in preparation to raise the aircraft is visible above the fuselage behind the cockpit.**

assembly line in May 1942 and made its first flight in July that year. The massive widened propulsion unit, consisting of two coupled DB 601E units mounted side by side driving a single set of four-bladed VDM airscrews, delivered 2,700hp at 2,700rpm on take-off. Even though it represented a respectable increase in power, this powerplant was nevertheless an emergency stopgap. Since no major problems were encountered with the DB 606 during flight trials, the V14 underwent considerable testing. A novelty with this prototype was the B-Stand FDL 131Z armament installation that was scheduled to be fitted to the V12 that followed it.

Ju 288 V13

Likewise powered by DB 606A/B powerplants, the V13 (DF+CS) flew for the first time in September 1942. It was equipped with a four-man pressurised cabin and weapon installations

including a new H-Stand in the fuselage tail. During its brief flying life it served mainly as a weapons test aircraft, until 16th May 1943 when it crash-landed due to engine problems. It suffered considerable damage and had to be written off.

Ju 288 V101

This prototype designation simply represents the last three digits of its *Werknummer* 2880101 and would normally have been identified as the V15 in the series. The V101 (BG+GX), the first prototype of the planned Ju 288C version, made its maiden flight on 30th October 1942. Like the preceding prototypes, it was powered by the DB 606A/B and had a pressurised cabin for a crew of four. On this machine, a fifth crew member was added as the tail gunner in the manned H-Stand equipped with 4 x MG 131s in the HL 131V quadruple mounting.

Top left: **Used on tail armament trials until this accident, the V13 crew compartment is here being hoisted separately from the fuselage by the lifting crane.**

Lower left: **The point of severance between the cockpit and the fuselage proper is clearly visible in this view of the V13.**

Top right: **The curved trail in the cornfield made by the V13 is apparent behind the fuselage. At upper right is a pylon that supported high-voltage overhead cables running across its path.**

Lower right: **A view of the pilot's area inside the Ju 288 V13 cockpit.**

Above left: **The Ju 288 V101 was the first prototype of the Ju 288C model, first flown on 30th October 1942. In the background is the Ju 288 V5.**

Above right: **The V101 fuselage centre section, seen from the rear.**

Right: **Inside the cockpit of the Ju 288 V102. DB 610-powered Ju 288C-Series Prototypes**

Right and below right: **Serving as a prototype for the planned Ju 288C-1 series, the V103 is seen (upper photo) in its original environment, and (lower photo) with the background airbrushed out.**

Top and centre left: **The V103 was powered by coupled DB 610 engines that necessitated widening the nacelles. In the He 177, these coupled units were the source of considerable problems. These photos show that the V103 has not yet received its full armament complement.**

Above right: **The central rectangular fuselage box of the V104. Equipped with DB 610A/B engines, it was fitted with strengthened dive-brakes.**

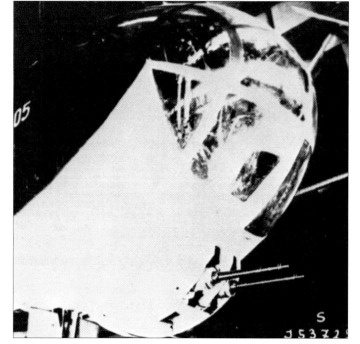

Left: **The movable twin MG 131Z machine-guns in the C1-Stand chin turret are clearly visible on the V105.**

Ju 288 Prototype Data Table

Prototype for model	Werk-Nr	Registration civil	military	Powerplant type	take-off power	Propellers -bladed	type	Span, m (ft)	Length, m (ft)	Height, m (ft)	Wing area m² (ft²)	Crew	First Flight
V1	2880001	D-AACS	-	2 x BMW 801G	1,730hp	3	VDM	18.37m (60' 3¼")	16.45m (53' 11⅝")	4.70m (15' 1")	54 (581.23)	3	29.11.40
V2	2880002	D-ABWP	BG+GR	2 x BMW 801G	1,730hp	3	VDM	20.20m (66' 3¼")	16.45m (53' 11⅝")	4.70m (15' 1")	59 (635.06)	3	01.03.41
V3	2880003	D-ACTF	BG+GS	2 x BMW 801G	1,730hp	3	VDM	22.00m (72' 2⅛")	16.45m (53' 11⅝")	4.70m (15' 1")	60 (645.83)	3	18.04.41
V4	2880004	D-ADVR	BG+GT	2 x BMW 801G	1,730hp	3	VDM	20.20m (66' 3¼")	16.45m (53' 11⅝")	4.70m (15' 1")	59 (635.06)	3	17.05.41
V5	2880005	D-A......	BG+GU	2 x Jumo 222A/B	2,000hp	4	VS7	18.37m (60' 3¼")	16.45m (53' 11⅝")	4.70m (15' 1")	54 (581.23)	3	08.10.41
V6 (A)	2880006	D-AFDN	BG+GV	2 x Jumo 222A/B	2,000hp	4	VS7	22.60m (74' 1¾")	18.10m (59' 4⅝")	5.00m (16' 4⅞")	64.7 (696.42)	3	18.01.42*
V7 (A)	2880007	-	BG+GW	2 x BMW 801C	1,600hp	3	VDM	22.60m (74' 1¾")	18.10m (59' 4⅝")	5.00m (16' 4⅞")	64.7 (696.42)	3	.07.42
V8 (A)	2880008	-	RD+MU	2 x Jumo 222A/B	2,000hp	4	VS7	22.60m (74' 1¾")	18.10m (59' 4⅝")	5.00m (16' 4⅞")	64.7 (696.42)	4	03.09.42*
V9 (B)	2880009	-	VE+QP	2 x Jumo 222A/B†	2,000hp	4	VS7	22.60m (74' 1¾")	18.10m (59' 4⅝")	5.00m (16' 4⅞")	64.7 (696.42)	4	02.05.42
V10 (B)	2880010	-	DF+CP	2 x BMW 801TJ	1,810hp	3	VDM	22.60m (74' 1¾")	18.10m (59' 4⅝")	5.00m (16' 4⅞")	64.7 (696.42)	4	30.01.43*
V11 (B)	2880011	D-ANXN	DF+CQ	2 x DB606A/B	2,700hp	4	VDM	22.60m (74' 1¾")	18.10m (59' 4⅝")	5.00m (16' 4⅞")	64.7 (696.42)	4	.07.42
V12 (A/B)	2880012	-	DF+CR	2 x Jumo 222A/B	2,000hp	4	VS7	22.60m (74' 1¾")	18.10m (59' 4⅝")	5.00m (16' 4⅞")	64.7 (696.42)	3	.06.42
V13 (B)	2880013	-	DF+CS	2 x DB606A/B	2,000hp	4	VDM	22.60m (74' 1¾")	18.10m (59' 4⅝")	5.00m (16' 4⅞")	64.7 (696.42)	4	.09.42
V14 (B)	2880014	-	DF+CT	2 x Jumo 222A/B	2,000hp	4	VS7	22.60m (74' 1¾")	18.10m (59' 4⅝")	5.00m (16' 4⅞")	64.7 (696.42)	4	09.11.42*
V101 (C)	2880101	-	BG+GX	2 x DB606A/B	2,700hp	4	VDM	22.60m (74' 1¾")‡	18.15m (59' 6½")	5.00m (16' 4⅞")	64.7 (696.42)	4	30.10.42
V102 (C)	2880102	-	BG+BY	2 x DB606A/B	2,700hp	4	VDM	22.60m (74' 1¾")‡	18.15m (59' 6½")	5.00m (16' 4⅞")	64.7 (696.42)	4	.01.43
V103 (C)	2880103	-	DE+ZZ	2 x DB610A/B	2,950hp	4	VDM	22.60m (74' 1¾")‡	18.15m (59' 6½")	5.00m (16' 4⅞")	64.7 (696.42)	4	13.08.43*
V104 (C)	2880104	-	-	2 x DB610A/B	2,950hp	4	VDM	22.60m (74' 1¾")‡	18.15m (59' 6½")	5.00m (16' 4⅞")	64.7 (696.42)	4	12.11.43*
V105	2880105	-	-	2 x DB610A/B	2,950hp	4	VDM	22.60m (74' 1¾")‡	18.15m (59' 6½")	5.00m (16' 4⅞")	64.7 (696.42)	4	.05.43
V106	2880106	-	BS+CA	2 x DB610A/B	2,950hp	4	VDM	22.60m (74' 1¾")‡	18.15m (59' 6½")	5.00m (16' 4⅞")	64.7 (696.42)	4	17.05.43*
V107	2880107	-	BS+CB	2 x DB610A/B	2,950hp	4	VDM	22.60m (74' 1¾")‡	18.15m (59' 6½")	5.00m (16' 4⅞")	64.7 (696.42)	4	.06.43
V108	2880108	-	BS+CC	2 x DB610A/B	2,950hp	4	VDM	22.60m (74' 1¾")‡	18.15m (59' 6½")	5.00m (16' 4⅞")	64.7 (696.42)	4	09.10.43

*First documented flight. †Later replaced by 2 x 2,500hp Jumo 222C/D (take-off power = 2,500hp). ‡Works drawing shows span 22.99m (75ft 1⅛in) and wing area 65m² (699.64ft²). The take-off power for the Jumo 222E/F = 2,500hp.

Ju 288 V102

The V102 (BG+GY) is generally described in aviation literature as having been powered by the DB 606A/B. One publication,* however, lists it in this connection with the DB 610 (2 x DB 605s). It was the second prototype for the Ju 288C-series and was broadly similar to the V101, having the same overall dimensions. The maiden flight took place in June 1943. It is presumed to have also been equipped with a manned H-Stand and HL 131V tail turret.

*Hugo Junkers – Pionier der Luftfahrt: Wolfgang Wagner; Bernard & Graefe Verlag, Bonn, 1996, p.461.

Ju 288 V103

The V103 (DE+ZZ), powered by two DB 610A/B motors, served as a model for the Ju 288C-1. The aircraft, which made its first flight in the spring of 1943, was inspected by Hermann Göring. Problems that had been encountered with the V101 and V102 were eliminated with this aircraft – the first Ju 288 to have fully equipped weapon stations. These consisted of a B-Stand (1 x MG 131Z), C1-Stand (1 x MG 131Z), C2-Stand (1 x MG 131Z) and H-Stand (1 x FHL 151) as well as stations for underwing.

Ju 288 V104

The V104 was a further prototype for the Ju 288C-1 and is said to have made its first flight in May 1943. As with the V105, the Luftwaffe call-sign assigned to it is not known. Armament and underwing stations were identical to those listed above for the V103, this prototype featuring altered dive-brakes.

Ju 288 V105

With the exception of minor details, this prototype was otherwise identical to its predecessor and flew for the first time in May 1943.

Ju 288 V106

First flown in May 1943, the V106 (BS+CA) similar to the V105 except for minor details. Documentary evidence exists of flights conducted between 17th May and 2nd October 1943.

Ju 288 V107

The maiden flight of the V107 (BS+CB) followed one month later than the preceding prototypes. Further flights have been documented for the period 23rd July to 27th November 1943. In July 1943 it suffered an undercarriage collapse on landing but was repaired. It is known that the aircraft was fitted with a C1-Stand chin turret and a B-Stand (FDL 131Z), but no confirmation is to hand as to whether its full armament was installed. Attachments for underwing weapons were probably also fitted.

Ju 288 V108

The last of the prototypes in this Werknummer series, the V108 (BS+CC) flew for the first time on 9th October 1943. Trials continued until May 1944 when it was lost through engine and undercarriage damage. In overall appearance it corresponded to its predecessors.

To summarise: When the test series ended in mid-1944, 17 of the 23 prototypes had suffered damage and had to be scrapped. Only 5 prototypes survived the wide-ranging and, from the material aspect, exceedingly strenuous flight-testing. All other airframes that were under construction were also to be scrapped. The three remaining V201 to V203 prototypes were handed over to the Luftwaffe which modified them in its own workshops to carry large-calibre armament or for other special tasks.

Ju 288 V201-V203

The precise Werknummer series for these aircraft remains unknown. The V201 was equipped in a Luftwaffe workshop with a recoilless cannon designed by Rheinmetall-Borsig of no less than 365mm (14.4in) calibre whose energy was dissipated immediately on firing as it would otherwise have destroyed the aircraft. The projectile itself, illustrated in a Junkers drawing dated February 1943, weighed 400kg (882 lb) and could be fired from a distance of up to 4,000m (4,372 yards) from the target. It was based on the MK 113 ordnance, but in a much deadlier form. A similar project had already been discussed in 1940/41 for the Ju 288G.

It is known that the other two prototypes had been fitted for the anti-tank role with the 5cm (2in) BK 5 (KWK 39) cannon in a similar manner to that installed in the Ju 88P. The aircraft were even said to have been put into action on the Eastern Front – a report that belongs to the realm of fantasy?

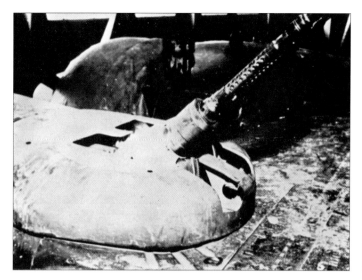

Top left: **The B-Stand weapon position aft of the cockpit on the V106, first flown in May 1943.**

Top right, above left and above right: **The V108 after damage to both the powerplant and undercarriage. The starboard propellers have already been removed, but three of its bent port propellers are still in place. In the lowest picture, the inward-canted twin endplate fins and rudders are clearly recognisable.**

Left: **The V107 seen during undercarriage tests.**

Chapter Three

The Planned Ju 288-Series Versions

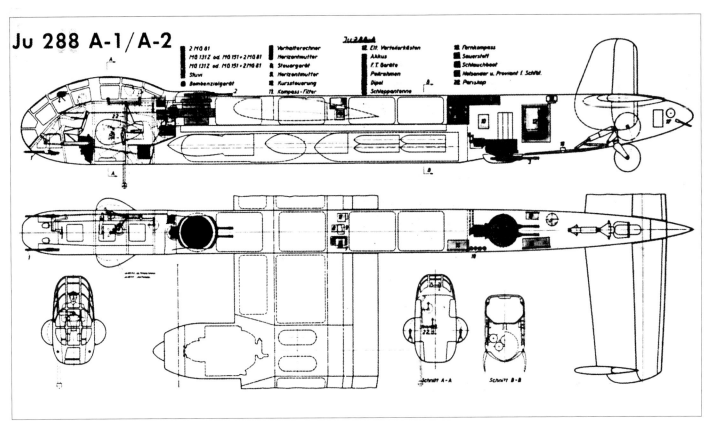

Ju 288 A-1/A-2

Detailed views of the Ju 288A-1 and A-2 internal installations.

Ju 288A

The first aircraft to appear in this configuration was the Ju 288 V5. This machine, together with successive prototypes and the Ju 288A, was to have been powered by two 2,000hp Jumo 222 engines, but as already described, only the prototypes were fitted with these, so the Ju 288A despite all its enthusiastic production plans came to nothing. We shall now turn to the technical details of this model.

In terms of dimensions and weights, the Ju 288A version was the smallest and lightest. The fuselage's narrow girth of 0.99m (39in) was just wide enough to accommodate its crew of three, and it had an overall length of 16.6m (54ft 5½in). Wingspan was 22m (72ft 4⅛in) and wing area was 60m² (645.82ft²). It had an equipped weight of 11,000kg (24,351 lb), rising by 6,300kg (13,889 lb) to its take-off weight of 17,300kg (38,140 lb). The next version was to have weighed up to 4,500kg (9,921 lb) more. With a maximum speed of 645km/h at 6,000m

(401mph at 19,685ft) the Ju 288A was 20km/h (12mph) faster than the Ju 288B, and having a range of 3,850km (2,392 miles) and a service ceiling of 10,300m (33,790ft), it was noticeably more effective than its heavier successor. More details concerning the technology of the Ju 288 are provided in the next chapter.

Ju 288B

This version was also built only in the form of five prototypes. Powerplants were likewise to have consisted of the Jumo 222, but with the more powerful 2,500hp E/F variants. The most important features of the Ju 288B, represented by the V14 prototype were:

- A fuselage length increased to 18.1m (59ft 4⅜in). Although the oval cross-section was retained, the cockpit area was widened to accommodate a crew of four in the pressurised cabin, giving the aircraft a completely different form compared with the bulged side blisters of the Ju 288A.
- During the course of development of the Ju 288B, exemplified by the V14, the empennage section was considerably modified, the twin fins and rudders being altered in shape and canted

inwards instead of being vertical as on the Ju 288A. On this version, the rudders extended the whole length of the fins so that their overall length was increased, this change having been introduced on the V8 prototype. The tail cone of the previous model was now replaced by a remote-controlled MG 151 tail barbette.

- The wing also differed considerably in plan form from that of the Ju 288A, the outboard wing leading edges forming a continuous straight line to the wingtips as against the double taper of its predecessor. The new wing, of aspect ratio 7.9, had a span of 22.6m (74ft 1¾in) and an area of 64.7m² (696.41ft²), this wing having been introduced on the V6 to V8 prototypes. These alterations necessitated a change in design to the ailerons and landing flaps. The dive-brakes were also drastically altered as seen in the upper three-view drawing on page.23. The previously more curved wing trailing edge contours gave way to one with straight sections.
- The powerplants, as already mentioned, were to have been the more powerful 2,500hp Jumo 222E/F, but which suffered from the same problems as the 2,000hp Jumo 222A/B. The

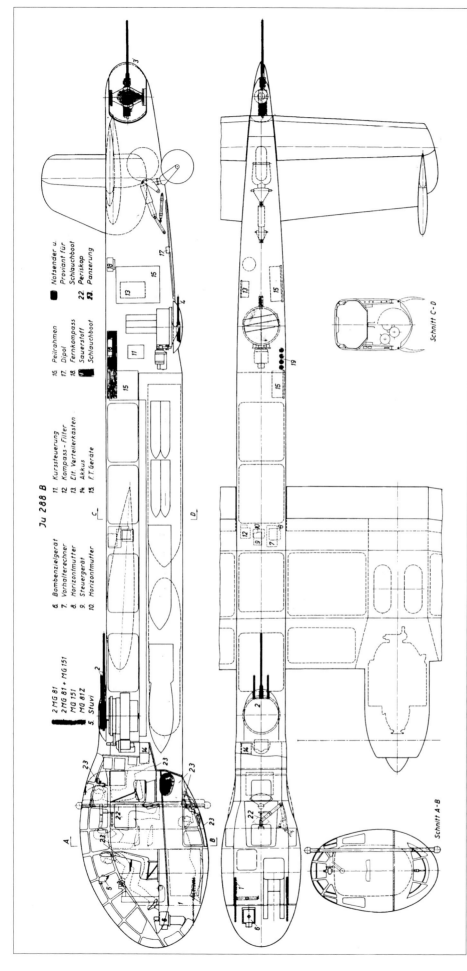

Ju 288 B

1. 2 MG 81
2. 2 MG 81 + MG 151
3. MG 151
4. MG 81Z
5. Stuvi
6. Bombenzielgerät
7. Vorhalterechner
8. Horizontmutter
9. Steuergerät
10. Horizontmutter
11. Kurssteuerung
12. Kompass - Filter
13. Elt Verteilerkasten
14. Akkus
15. F.T. Geräte
16. Peilrahmen
17. Dipol
18. Fernkompass
■ Schlauchboot
22. Periskop
▨. Panzerung
■ Notsender u. Proviant für Schlauchboot
Sauerstoff

Schnitt C - D

Schnitt A - B

sub-designations A/B and E/F indicated that the four-bladed VS 7 airscrews on the port and starboard nacelles rotated in opposite directions.

- On the Ju 288A and Ju 288B, the fuel load was housed in six protected wing tanks made up of 2 x 720 litres, 2 x 660 litres and 2 x 400 litres, and four fuselage tanks each of 450 litres, making a total of 5,360 litres. The 83 octane B4 fuel was first pumped from the others into the two fuselage forward feed tanks. To increase the range, two jettisonable tanks each of 900 litres could be carried on underwing stations that could also be used for bombs. With these, total fuel capacity was 7,160 litres.

- The 460 litres of lubricant oil was housed in two wing tanks each of 230 litres capacity in the wing centre section. According to a three-view drawing of the Ju 288A prepared at a later date, these fuel and lubricant quantities were also valid for the Ju 288B.

- The rolling components of the Ju 288B comprised twin mainwheels each of 1,015 x 380mm (40 x 15in) diameter and width on either side of a single oleo leg whose centres were located 5.5m (18ft 0½in) apart. The higher weight of this model required larger mainwheels than the 935 x 345mm (36.8 x 13.6in) of the Ju 288A, but with no other major alterations in this area. The Ju 288B and C each had a tailwheel measuring 630 x 220mm (24.80 x 8.67in) that could be swivelled through 90°, all undercarriage members being hydraulically extended and retracted.

- The military equipment of the Ju 288B was significantly increased over that of the Ju 288A. The armament fitted to the prototypes varied greatly. Initially, the Ju 288B was to have had an MG 131Z in the B- and C-Stands, with 1 x MG 151 in the tail H-Stand. In a later variant, the B-Stand was to have 2 x MG 81s plus 1 x MG 151, and 1 x MG 131Z each in the C- and H-Stands respectively. A combination of various bombloads could be carried internally, without modification to the bomb bay, up to a maximum of 3,000kg (6,614 lb).

Ju 288C

This was to have been the third series-version of the same design, Professor Hertel having again made several alterations including a renewed airframe and powerplant changes. At this stage, however, it had little in common with the original concept of the 'Bomber B'. The corresponding Ju 288C configuration was to have been tested with the V101 to V108 prototypes, but even these differed considerably in their fittings and equipment. In all, three variants had been drawn up: the Ju 288C-1, C-2 and C-3, whose series manufacture was to remain no more than wishful thinking. In contrast to the Ju 288B, the Ju 288C had the following distinguishing features:

- Fuselage length was increased over that of the Ju 288B to 18.15m (59ft 6½in), together with a strengthening of the structure.

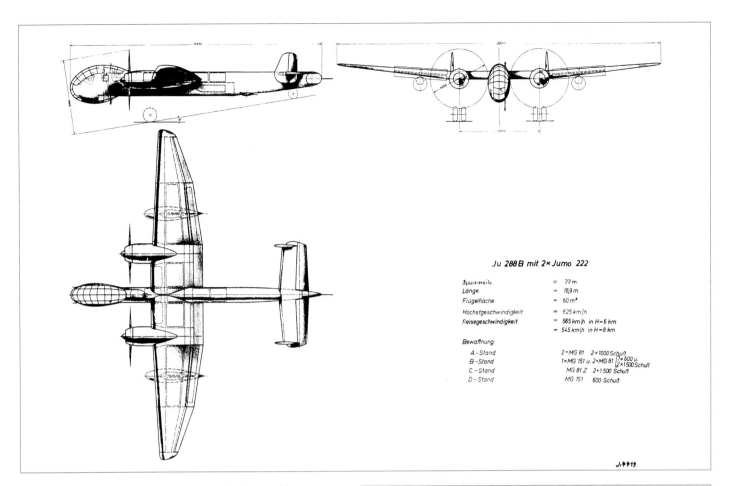

Ju 288 B mit 2×Jumo 222

Spannweite	= 22 m
Länge	= 16,9 m
Flügelfläche	= 60 m²
Höchstgeschwindigkeit	= 625 km/h
Reisegeschwindigkeit	= 565 km/h in H=6 km
	= 545 km/h in H=8 km

Bewaffnung:

A–Stand	2×MG 81	2×1000 Schuß
B–Stand	1×MG 151 u. 2×MG 81	1×600 u. 2×1500 Schuß
C–Stand	MG 81 Z	2×1500 Schuß
D–Stand	MG 151	600 Schuß

Above: **Ju 288B three-view drawing. Details include: span 22m (72ft 2⅛in), length 16.97m (55ft 8⅛in), height 5m (16ft 4⅞in), wing area 60m² (645.82ft²), maximum speed 625km/h (388mph), cruising speeds 565km/h at 6km (351mph at 19,685ft) and 545km/h at 8km (339mph at 26,250ft). Armament and number of rounds for each are listed below.**

Right: **The Ju 288C-1 with DB 610 engines. Notice the altered wing plan form in comparison with the Ju 288B.**

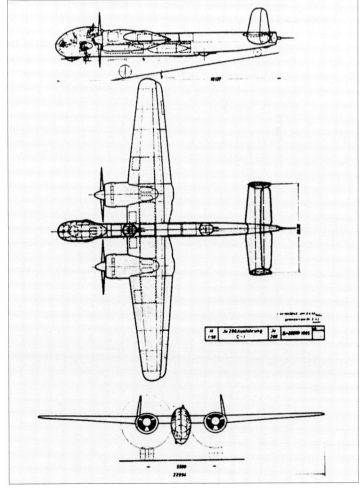

Illustration on the opposite page:
Cross-sectional details of the Ju 288B with 2 x Jumo 222 engines.

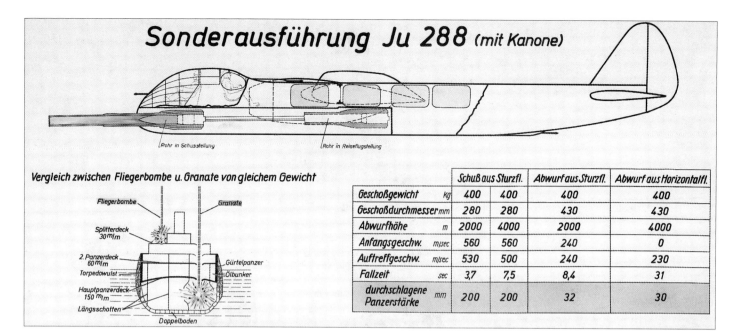

Sonderausführung Ju 288 (mit Kanone)

Rohr in Schussstellung *Rohr in Reiseflugstellung*

Vergleich zwischen Fliegerbombe u. Granate von gleichem Gewicht

Fliegerbombe — Granate
Splitterdeck 30 m/m
2. Panzerdeck 60 m/m — Gürtelpanzer
Torpedowulst — Ölbunker
Hauptpanzerdeck 150 m/m
Längsschotten
Doppelboden

		Schuß aus Sturzfl.		Abwurf aus Sturzfl.	Abwurf aus Horizontalfl.
Geschoßgewicht	kg	400	400	400	400
Geschoßdurchmesser	mm	280	280	430	430
Abwurfhöhe	m	2000	4000	2000	4000
Anfangsgeschw.	m/sec	560	560	240	0
Auftreffgeschw.	m/sec	530	500	240	230
Fallzeit	sec	3,7	7,5	8,4	31
durchschlagene Panzerstärke	mm	200	200	32	30

- The high-altitude pressurised cabin for the crew of four remained unchanged; apart from minor alterations, as did the empennage area.
- The wing, on the other hand, underwent considerable alterations as can be seen in the accompanying Ju 288C drawing. Wingspan was to have been increased later to 22.99m (75ft 5⅛in) and wing area to 65m² (699.64ft²), this alteration being confirmed in a works drawing. In other publications, a span of 22.6m (74ft 1¾in) has been quoted, this figure being most probably that adopted for all the V-models described earlier. The wing-mounted dive-brakes were also strengthened.
- In the Ju 288C, the alternative or 'fall-back' powerplant was the DB 610A/B, a 2,950hp coupled unit driving four-bladed VDM propellers that was responsible in the He 177 for not only considerable anxieties but also several fatal accidents. In the course of the Ju 288 programme, however, the pilots expressed in varying degrees a generally high opinion of the reliability of the DB 610 – a motor that had the significant disadvantages of higher weight and increased frontal drag.
- The fuel system of the Ju 288C corresponded to that of the Ju 288B, but envisaged an increased total capacity of 8,650 litres which included two 900-litre drop-tanks and an increase in the total of lubricant carried.
- The undercarriage corresponded to that of the Ju 288B, but now supported a take-off weight of 21,800kg (48,060 lb) compared with the 17,300kg (38,140 lb) of the Ju 288A and the 21,200kg (46,738 lb) of the Ju 288B. On the Ju 288B and C, mainwheel dimensions were identical.
- For the Ju 288C, corresponding to the C-1 variant, defensive armament was again increased, consisting of 1 x MG 81Z in each of the B-, C1- and C2-Stands, and 1 x MG 151 in the H-Stand. Internal bombloads were the same as in the earlier versions.

On the other Ju 288C models, defensive armament was made up as follows:
- Ju 288C-2: 2 x MG 151s in each of the B-, C1- and C2-Stands and 1 x HL 131V (or alternatively 1 x FHL 131Z) in the H-Stand.
- Ju 288C-3: This projected night bomber variant, otherwise similar to the C-1, was to have had only 1 x MG 131Z in the ventral C2-Stand.

With the Ju 288C models, planning had by no means come to an end, as mention must be made of the Ju 288D and G, and the Ju 288 *Höhenbomber* (high-altitude bomber).

Ju 288D
This version was for a heavily armed bomber, envisaged with the more powerful 3,100hp DB 610C/D units. The armament comprised 1 x MG 131Z in each of the B-, C1- and C2-Stands, with the tail armament strengthened to 4 x MG 131s in the HL 131V manual tail turret which increased the crew to five. Dimensions for the Ju 288D were the same as the Ju 288C.

This designation has often been applied to those remaining Ju 288 prototypes that had been converted for the anti-tank role. However, this was never an official type designation and is incorrect as these prototypes were not allocated a new identity in the form of a sub-type letter.

Ju 288G (for Gerät 104)
This designation existed on the drawing board at Junkers during the period 1940/41 and was applied to a variant equipped with the large-calibre Gerät 104 'Münchhausen' cannon, intended for attacks on shipping. Having a calibre of no less than 355mm (14in), it took the form of a recoilless gun barrel housed within the aircraft's fuselage and was extended from the nose when set up for firing its 400kg (882 lb) shell. This was capable of penetrating 400mm (15.75in) of armour plating at a velocity of 405m/sec (1,329ft/sec = 906mph).

Wether this technically interesting configuration made it into service is questionable.

The accompanying drawing of a further scheme has also survived. In this instance, the recoilless cannon with a calibre of 280mm (11in) was known as the Düka 280 (from *Düsenkanone* = jet cannon). As shown in the accompanying illustration of the Ju 288 special variant, the shell, equipped with a delayed-action fuse, was capable of inflicting enormous damage deep inside the bowels of a ship after penetrating several layers of amour-plated decks compared with a standard air-dropped bomb. The 400kg (882 lb) projectile, when fired in a dive at 2,000m (6,560ft) at an initial velocity of 560m/sec (1,837ft/sec), attained an impact velocity of 530m/sec (1,739ft/sec) 3.7 seconds later, penetrating 200mm (7.9in) of armour plating. When fired in a dive from an altitude of 4,000m (13,120ft), corresponding impact velocity was 500m/sec (1,640ft/sec) and flight time 7.5 seconds. This, at least, was the theory. Whether this monstrous cannon would have proven itself in reality is doubtful: only a single shot was possible per sortie, since no reloading mechanism is visible on the drawing. The imagination of the engineers in this case produced extraordinary expectations.

Ju 288 *Höhenbomber* with Jumo 222
The most notable feature of this high-altitude bomber variant intended to be powered by the Jumo 222A/B was undoubtedly its increase in wingspan to 26m (85ft 3⅜in) and fuselage length to 18.095m (59ft 4⅜in) for the crew of four in the pressurised cabin. Equipped weight was 11,000kg (24,251 lb). With a payload consisting of 2,800kg (6,173 lb) of fuel and a 2,000kg (4,409 lb) bombload, take-off weight was 16,500kg (36,376 lb). Performance calculations gave a maximum speed of 680km/h at 11,000m (423mph at 36,090ft), a range of

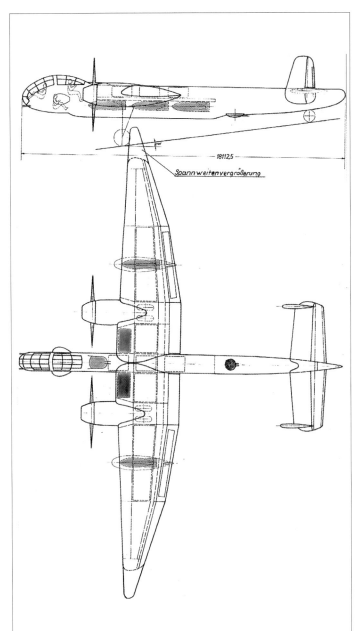

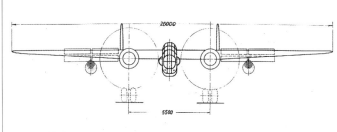

Höhenbomber Ju 288

Bewaffnung

A–Stand : 2 × MG 81 mit 2 × 500 Schuss
B–Stand : MG 81Z 2 × 750 "
C–Stand : " " "

Motoren : 2 × BMW 801 J,K

Startleistung 2 × 1480 PS
Kampfleistung 2 × 1220 PS in H = 12 km

Rüstgewicht	kg	9900
Kraftstoff	"	2000
Bombenlast	"	1000
Abfluggewicht	"	13500
Vmax in H 12 km	km/h	650
Reisehöhe	km	12
Technische Flugstrecke	"	1800
bei V Reise	km/h	615
H Dienst	km	14

Left and above: **The Ju 288 high-altitude bomber with BMW 801J or K.**

Below: **This Ju 288 proposal powered by the Jumo 223 existed only on the drawing board. Note the single fin and rudder, the whole aircraft resembling the EF 73 project.**

Ju 288 mit 223

Startleistung 2500 PS   Kampfleistung 1650 PS

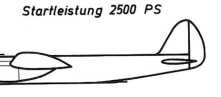

Reisegeschwindigk. in 6 km Höhe   580 km/h
Höchstgeschwindigk. in 6 km Höhe   650 km/h

Reichweite km	2500	3500	4500	5000
Bombenlast kg	3000	1500	1000	500

2,400km (1,491 miles) at cruising speed 590km/h (367mph) and a service ceiling of 13,000m (42,650ft). Defensive armament consisted of 1 x MG 81Z in each of the B-, C- and H-Stands.

Ju 288 *Höhenbomber* with BMW 801

This Ju 288 high-altitude bomber variant, powered by BMW 801J or K engines each of 1,480hp at take-off and 1,220hp at 12,000m (39,370ft), had correspondingly lower weights and performance than the Jumo 222-powered version but with a higher service ceiling. Compared to the Jumo 222-powered variant described above, equipped weight was 9,900kg (21,826 lb), fuel 2,000kg (4,409 lb), bombload 1,000kg (2,205 lb) and take-off weight 13,500kg (29,762 lb). Maximum speed was 650km/h at cruising altitude 12,000m (39,370ft), range 1,800km at 615km/h (1,118 miles at 382mph) and service ceiling 14,000m (45,930ft). Wingspan and undercarriage track were the same as the Jumo 222-powered variant, except

that the drawing shows an overall length of 18.1125m (59ft 5⅛in). Armament is as shown in the data below the drawing.

Ju 288 with Jumo 223

The Jumo 223 diesel engine of 2,500hp at take-off and combat power of 1,650hp was foreseen as an alternative powerplant to the Jumo 222E/F. As shown in the drawing, estimated performance for this variant was as follows:

- maximum speed: 650km/h at 6,000m (404mph at 19,685ft)
- cruising speed: 580km/h at 6,000m (360mph at 19,685ft)
- range with 3,000kg (6,614 lb) bombload: 2,500km (1,553 miles)
- range with 1,500kg (3,307 lb) bombload: 3,500km (2,175 miles)
- range with 1,000kg (2,205 lb) bombload: 4,500km (2,796 miles)
- range with 500kg (1,102 lb) bombload: 5,000km (3,107 miles).

Junkers Ju 288-Series Data Comparison

	EF 73	Ju 288A	Ju 288B	Ju 288C
Powerplant				
Designation	Jumo 222A/B	Jumo 222A/B	Jumo 222E/F	DB 610A/B
Take-off power	2 x 2,000hp	2 x 2,000hp	2 x 2,500hp	2 x 2,950hp
Airscrews	4 x VS 7	4 x VS 7	4 x VS 7	4 x VDM
Dimensions				
Wingspan	15.70m (51' 6⅛")	22.00m (72' 2⅛")	22.60m (74' 1¾")	22.60m (74' 1¾")†
Length	16.10m (52' 9⅞")	16.60m (54' 5½")	18.10m (59' 4⅝")	18.15m (59' 6½")
Heigh	4.50m (14' 9⅛")	4.60m (15' 1⅛")	5.00m (16' 4⅞")	5.00m (16' 4⅞")
Wing area, m² (ft²)	54.70 (588.77)	60.00 (645.82)	64.70 (696.41)	64.70 (696.41)
Weights				
Equipped weight, kg (lb)	8,100 (17,857)	11,000 (24,251)	13,600 (29,983)	13,000 (28,660)
Fuel capacity, litres (gals)	4,010 (882)	7,160 (1,575)	7,160 (1,575)	8,650 (1,903)
Take-off weight, kg (lb)	13,400 (29,542)	17,300 (38,140)	21,200 (46,738)	21,800 (48,060)
Take-off wing loading, kg/m (lbft²)	245 (50.17)	288 (59.06)	328 (67.11)	227 (69.01)
Performance:				
Maximum speed	650km/h at 6,400m 404mph at 21,000ft	645km/h at 6,000m 401mph at 19,685ft	625km/h at 6,000m 388mph at 19,685ft	655km/h at 6,800m 407mph at 22,310ft
Cruising speed	500km/h at 6,400m 311mph at 21,000ft	565km/h at 6,000m 351mph at 19,685ft	545km/h at 6,000m 339mph at 19,685ft	520km/h at 6,800m 323mph at 22,310ft
Range, km (miles)	3,000 (1,864)	3,850 (2,392)	3,600 (2,237)	2,800 (1,740)
Service ceiling, m (ft)	8,800 (28,870)	10,300 (33,790)	9,400 (30,640)	10,370 (34,020)
Armament:				
Nose, fixed	2 x MG 81	-	-	-
A-Stand	-	2 x MG 81	-	-
B-Stand	1 x MG 81Z	1 x MG 131Z	1 x MG 131Z*	1 x MG 131Z
C-Stand	-	1 x MG 131Z	1 x MG 131Z*	-
C1-Stand	-	-	-	1 x MG 131Z
C2-Stand	1 x MG 81Z	-	-	1 x MG 131Z
H-Stand	-	1 x MG 151	1 x MG 151*	1 x MG 151
Bombload, kg (lb)	3,000 (6,614)	3,000 (6,614)	3,000 (6,614)	3,000 (6,614)
Crew	three	three	four	four

*Initial proposal. †Planned span expansion to 22.99m (75ft 5.1in) and wing area to 65m² (699.64ft²).

Chapter Four

Ju 288 Technical Details

In the design of the Ju 188, special emphasis was laid on a production-oriented type of construction as well as high structural strength coupled with the greatest possible reduction in weight. The fuselage with its rectangular cross-section was built in three main segments: the pressurised crew compartment (which if necessary could be easily separated from the centre fuselage); the centre fuselage section; and the rear fuselage that supported the empennage surfaces.

The trapezoidal shoulder-mounted wing, consisting of a centre and two outer sections, formed a central element with the fuselage. The components, described here only briefly, were of all-metal dural-skinned construction conforming to stress group H3. A technological highlight was the pressurised cabin, the technicalities of which were not fully understood at that time. Viewed as a whole, with the Ju 288, the Luftwaffe had at its disposal a technically advanced aircraft and, with the engines originally intended for it, one capable of very high performance. But even this representative of the 'Bomber B' programme in its three principal versions was not able to reach the series-production stage. The chief reasons for this were the constantly changing priorities and the difficulties surrounding the Jumo 222 powerplant.

We shall now examine the technicalities of this fascinating but regrettably unsuccessful Junkers design.

Cockpit

The so-called *Höhenkammer* (high-altitude chamber) formed the self-contained forward fuselage component attached to the main central structure by four quick-release bolts. Here, the cables and supply lines were also detachable. It was only through the introduction of this feature that such an aircraft could be created which was able to penetrate enemy airspace at high altitudes and was therefore more difficult to attack. But it was precisely this technology that presented problems for the designers and led all too often to them being bedevilled by technical hitches. Whereas Junkers had been able to draw on previous experience in the design and construction of the high-altitude

Ju 49, EF 61 or the Ju 86 reconnaissance aircraft, there were still several problems that needed to be solved in the Ju 288. In the course of its development, three versions were evolved: the Ju 288A for a crew of three, and the Ju 288B and C for a crew of four which necessitated a wider pressurised cabin.

The original design of the pressurised cabin formed an arched component ahead of the main fuselage structure. The large number of clear-vision panels provided the pilot at the centre with the best visibility. In the widened compartment, however, two crew members were seated side by side. The other two crew members, besides performing other tasks, had to operate the remote-controlled armament stands from their stations.

Cockpit Construction: The lower component formed the sheet metal trough, the upper forming the extensively glazed framework. The basic construction element consisted of four longitudinal frames which distributed the forces resulting from pressure differences to the stiffened frames. Added to these were the six transverse profiles that not only formed supporting elements for the skinning but also absorbed the resulting forces. The design was laid out for a pressure difference of 0.4kg/m². The upper glazed component consisted of a steel-framed structure that could absorb the excess pres-

sures in this region. The generous double-glazed Plexiglas panels had an outer layer thickness of 8mm and 2mm thickness for the inner. To counteract the build-up of moisture between the two layers, moisture-absorbing cartridges that served also as ventilators were installed. These produced a pressure equalisation between the panels and the inside of the cockpit, and thus compensated the bending loads acting upon the internal Plexiglas layer. In order to produce an aerodynamically optimal shape of the cockpit canopy, sharply curved vision-panel segments were unavoidable. To provide ideal sighting conditions, particularly near the pilot's position and weapon sights, the canopy panels were almost flat. Special glass was employed to aid astro-navigation. In the case of the three-man high-altitude chamber, two pressure-tight blisters were incorporated in the cockpit sides for installation of the gunsights.

The pressurised crew compartment itself was linked to the centre fuselage element at four attachment points on frame 6, the two upper joints being additionally braced (see drawing below). The overall length of this section was 4.17m (13ft 8⅛in). Crew protection was provided by armour plating of 10mm thickness for the head, 8mm for the head and chest, and 4mm for the seat, these features applying to all three major versions.

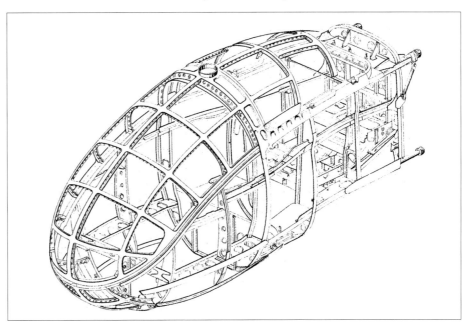

The structure of the Ju 288 high-altitude pressure cabin and its attachment points to the centre fuselage.

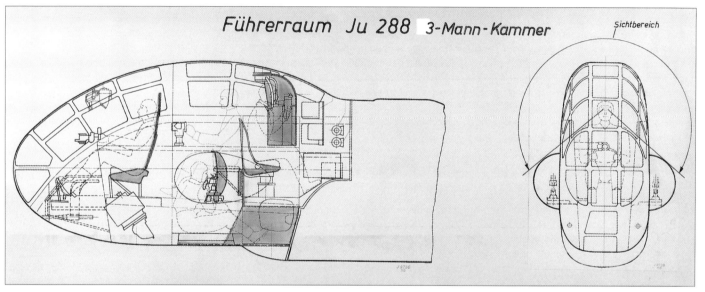

Führerraum Ju 288 3-Mann-Kammer

Sichtbereich

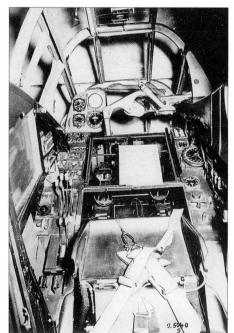

Arbeitsplatz des Flugzeugführers
Wegklappbarer Kartentisch
Rückenlehne zurückgelegt.

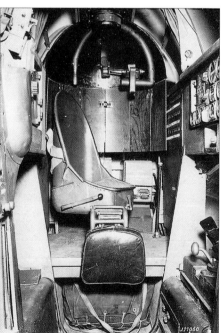

Arbeitsplatz des B-Standschützen
(Kopf- und Brustpanzerung)

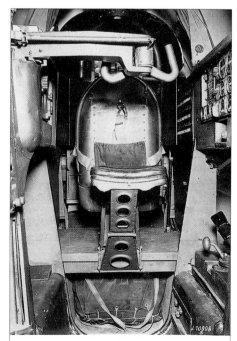

Oberer Sitz des C-Standschützen
mit heruntergeklappter Hilfssteuerung

J. 10121 SO

Opposite page:

Top left: **The upper bracing frames of the three-man pressurised cockpit seen here was made of steel.**

Top right: **This view shows the location of the upper periscopic sight on the Ju 288 V11 prototype.**

Centre: **Seating arrangement and pilot's field of vision in the three-crew pressurised cabin.**

Bottom left: **The pilot's area seen with its seat backrest moved rearward and which could be swivelled to one side.**

Bottom, centre: **The B-Stand gunner's position with head and chest armour plating.**

Bottom right: **The upper seat of the C-Stand gunner with control arm swung down to the horizontal position.**

The four views below show the Ju 288A forward pressurised compartment undergoing towing tests in Trebbichau Lake west of Dessau towards the end of 1941.

The radio operator's position with rear armour plating panels moved aside to the right

The BZG 2 bomb-aiming instrument in its operating position. When not in use, the bombsight was stowed beneath the pilot's seat.

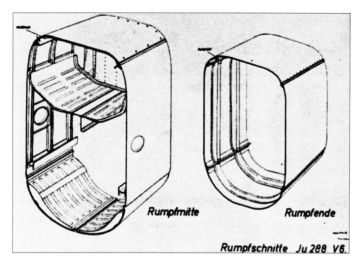

Rumpfmitte   Rumpfende

Rumpfschnitte Ju 288 V6.

Above: **Examples of the centre and rear fuselage construction on the Ju 288 V6.**

Right: **View inside the long bomb bay. The bomb door side hinges are clearly visible.**

Below: **Centre and rear fuselage of the Ju 288B-1 with numbered exchangeable parts.**

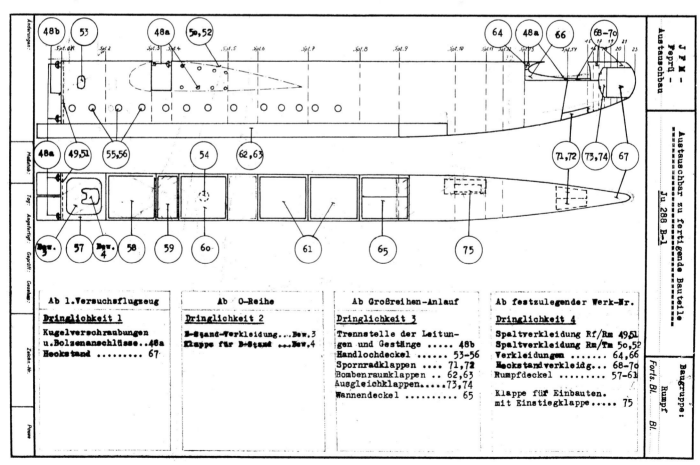

Ab 1.Versuchsflugzeug	Ab O-Reihe	Ab Großreihen-Anlauf	Ab festzulegender Werk-Nr.
Dringlichkeit 1	**Dringlichkeit 2**	**Dringlichkeit 3**	**Dringlichkeit 4**
Kugelverschraubungen u.Bolzenanschlüsse..48a	B-Stand-Verkleidung...Bew.3	Trennstelle der Leitungen und Gestänge 48b	Spaltverkleidung Rf/Rm 49,51
Heckstand 67	Klappe für B-Stand ...Bew.4	Handlochdeckel 53-56	Spaltverkleidung Rm/Tm 50,52
		Spornradklappen 71,72	Verkleidungen 64,66
		Bombenraumklappen .. 62,63	Heckstandverkleidg... 68-7o
		Ausgleichklappen.....73,74	Rumpfdeckel 57-61
		Wannendeckel 65	Klappe für Einbauten. mit Einstiegklappe..... 75

JFM - Feprü - Austauschbau

Austauschbar zu fertigende Bauteile

Ju 288 B-1

Baugruppe: Rumpf

Forts. Bl.   Bl.

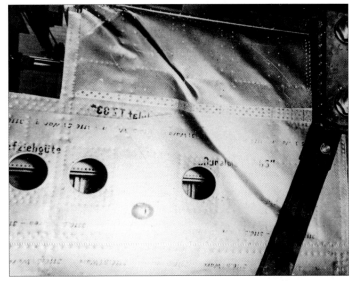

Above: **Crumpled fuselage skin panels resulting from load tests.**

Above right: **Early form of the endplate fins and rudders and fuselage tail end.**

Right: **The revised fin and rudder with upper compensating balance.**

Far right: **The same fin and rudder showing its thickness decreasing towards the top.**

Fuselage

Attached at its extremities to the cockpit and empennage, the fuselage centre section of 99cm (39in) width housed the majority of the fuel and military loads. Of all-metal semi-monocoque construction, it had an upper T-shaped main longeron, that beneath being of H-form. Torsionally rigid in its construction, it was made up of 23 transverse fuselage frames from front to rear and upper and lower loading bays separated by a mid-positioned flooring dividing the bomb bay from the fuel tank compartments. The bomb bay, capable of housing bombs of various types and calibres and extending over a length of 7.9m (25ft 11in), was enclosed by two full-length bomb doors that gave it an aerodynamically streamlined form.

The fuselage upper half housed a total of four fuel tanks each of 450 litres capacity, the bag-tanks being separated from each other by bulkheads. Access to the tanks was by means of maintenance hatches on the dorsal fuselage. This centre fuselage section also contained two remote-controlled weapon stands as well as parts of the radio installation, master compass and other electronic equipment, details of which are visible in the works drawings.

The attachment point to the tail assembly was at bulkhead 13. The rear fuselage section supporting the twin fins and rudders and housing the retractable tailwheel was made up of individual sheet skin panels attached to the transverse frames and Z-shaped stringers. The four tail section longeron extensions were

joined at the same attachment points to the four fuselage centre-section longerons, which enabled a quick exchange of this assembly component terminating in a tail cone or alternatively a tail barbette. For the Ju 288A fuselage, overall length was 16.6m (54ft 5½in); for the Ju 288B, 18.1m (59ft 4⅝in); and for the Ju 288C, 18.15m (59ft 6½in).

Empennage

The tail components exhibited a number of differences between the Ju 288A-series and successive development models, especially in respect of the twin fins and rudders. On the Ju 288A, these were both vertical, whereas on the Ju 288B and C, they were canted slightly inwards. The endplate rudders on the two latter models extended the whole length of the fin trailing edge, which was not the case with the Ju 288A, where the rudders were shorter in

length. On the Ju 288B, the rudders had internal horn balances and hence had no projecting surfaces at the extremities of the electrically operated control surfaces. In a Ju 288 drawing, tailspan is given as 7.11m (23ft 4in). Except for the wooden leading-edge profiles, the empennage was of all-metal construction.

Wing

This was made up of three major segments: the 6.67m (21ft 10⅜in) span centre section attached as a shoulder-mounted unit to the centre fuselage; and the two outer sections attached by universal joints to the engine transverse supports of the centre section, enabling the outer sections to be easily exchangeable. When required to fulfil a particular role, it was thus relatively easy to attach outer wings of longer span at these points. During its existence, various

Above: **Empennage detail on the Ju 288 V6 (D-AFDN).**

Above right: **In this view, the fins and rudders are vertical to the tailplane.**

Below: **This photograph shows the inward-canted fins and rudders with upper horn balances as on the Ju 288B. Powerplants are the wide-nacelle DB engines.**

wing configurations had either been built or were under development, as noted below:

- Ju 288A: span 22m (72ft 2⅛in), wing area 60m² (645.82ft²)
- Ju 288B: span 22.6m (74ft 1¾in), wing area 64.7m² (696.41ft²)
- Ju 288C: span 22.6m (74ft 1¾in), wing area 64.7m² (696.41ft²). This wingspan was later increased to 22.99m (75ft 5⅛in) and area to 65m² (699.64ft²) but was probably not applied to the prototypes.
- Ju 288 *Höhenbomber* (high-altitude bomber): span 26m (85ft 3⅜in).

The wing construction featured several major differences from other Junkers bomber designs. The reason for this lay in weight reduction as well as the use of spar stiffeners to avoid excessive skin wrinkling. On its outboard sections, the trapezoidal wing plan form had a slight taper on both leading and trailing edges towards the tips, with straight leading edges inboard of the engine nacelles. The basic load-bearing element of the outer sections was a one-piece main spar combined with two auxiliary spars. The wing was equipped with the so-called *Kutonase* barrage balloon cable-deflectors situated beneath the skin of the wing leading edge profile, as seen in the drawing. Split landing flaps were divided between both the centre and outer wing sections. The wing was slotted over its entire span and in construction was not dissimilar to the Ju 88. The lattice or slatted dive-brakes were attached to the outer landing flaps as shown in the plan-view drawing.

In addition to supporting the entire engine nacelles and main undercarriage members, the wing housed fuel and lubricant located in six bullet-proof fuel tanks with a total capacity

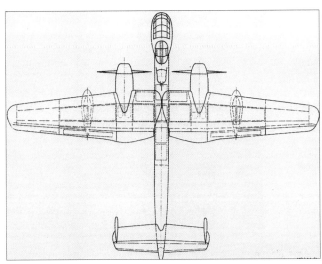

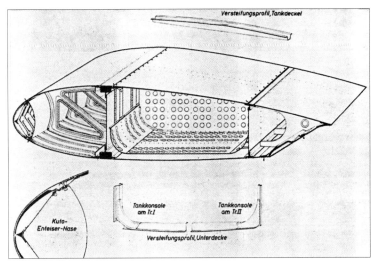

Above: **The Ju 288 wing plan form of span 22.6m (74ft 1¾in).**

Above right: **Examples of the wing structure, with nose cable-fenders and external wing stiffeners.**

Below: **The main fuselage segment and wing centre section. The upper open portions are the locations of the fuel and oil tanks.**

The so-called Kammunterbrecher (comb interruptors) that extended over the wings at 35% chord are seen here on the Ju 288 V5.

Unfortunately of poor quality, this photo nevertheless shows the slatted dive-brakes fitted to the Ju 288 V4 (D-ADVR).

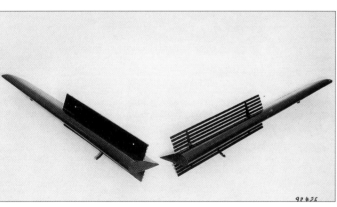

Two different types of dive-brakes that were developed – the closed surface at left, and the slatted type at right.

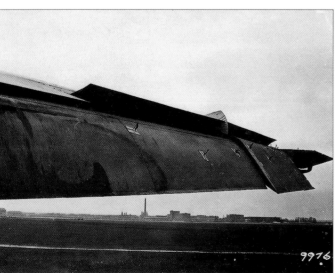

Details of control surfaces on the starboard wing trailing edge.

of 3,520 litres and two oil tanks each of 230 litres capacity. The latter were located ahead of the main spar in the wing centre section between the fuselage and engine nacelles. The fuel quantity carried could be increased by the addition of a 900-litre drop-tank located on the underwing station on each outboard wing section.

Ju 288-Series Powerplants

BMW 801: This 14-cylinder twin-row radial, proven on numerous occasions in operational use, was installed in a not insignificant number of aircraft types, among them the Fw 190, Do 217, Ju 290 and Ju 188. The first example was run on the static test-stand in the spring of 1939. It was the first German twin-row radial to be put into large-scale series production and incorporated experience gained in the design of the BMW 139 and Bramo 329 radials. Its 14 cylinders, arranged in two banks each of 7 cylinders, had a total capacity of 41.8 litres (2,550in³) and, depending upon the engine variant, delivered up to 2,000hp. The BMW 801G engine was installed in the Ju 288 V1 to V4, the BMW 801C in the V7, and the BMW 801TJ in the V10 prototype. This last-named model was a variant equipped with an exhaust-gas supercharger based on the BMW 801D-2, and was designated BMW 801J when installed in the Ju 288, the complete engine installation being known as the 9-8801-J0. A zero-series was manufactured from the beginning of 1944 under the designation BMW 801TJ (1,810hp) and was used as an emergency stopgap for the Jumo 222 in the Ju 388. Four prototypes of the Ju 288 were equipped with the BMW 801G of 1,730hp as against the 1,600hp BMW 801C which was a bomber engine used in the V7. Owing to the difference in output compared with the envisaged Jumo 222, the Ju 288 was not able to fulfil the expectations placed in it when powered by this motor.

Junkers-Jumo 222: The first Jumo 222-equipped prototype was the Ju 288 V5. Since it was more powerful than the BMW 801, an improvement in performance was demonstrated during the course of flight trials. Further prototypes equipped with this all-too-rare powerplant were the Ju 288 V6, V8, V9, V12 and V14, each fitted with the 2,000hp Jumo 222A/B. The more powerful successive engine variants that were expected to deliver 2,500hp and 3,000hp did not reach the installation stage. Performance calculations relative to the Ju 288 were nevertheless very encouraging. The high-altitude Jumo 222A-3/B-3 was installed, a variant with enlarged bore and stroke (140/135mm) which had already been a feature in the Jumo 222A-2/B-2, raising the power by 500hp to 2,500hp. Use of this powerplant in the Ju 288 was not confined to the Jumo 222A-1/B-1 but included the V9 prototype with the Jumo 222C/D variant.

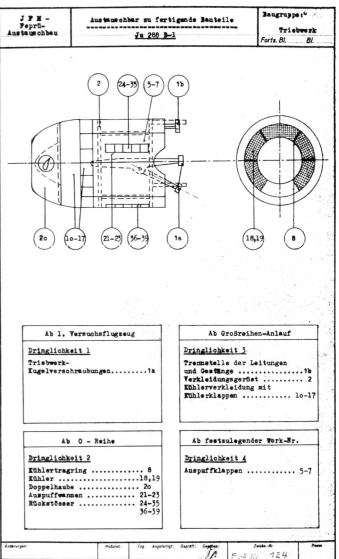

Ab 1. Versuchsflugzeug	Ab Großreihen-Anlauf
Dringlichkeit 1 Triebwerk- Kugelverschraubungen.........1a	**Dringlichkeit 3** Trennstelle der Leitungen und Gestänge ....1b Verkleidungsgerüst .... 2 Kühlerverkleidung mit Kühlerklappen 1o-17

Ab O - Reihe	Ab festzulegender Werk-Nr.
Dringlichkeit 2 Kühlertragring .... 8 Kühler ....18,19 Doppelhaube .... 2o Auspuffwannen .... 21-23 Rückstösser 24-35 36-39	**Dringlichkeit 4** Auspuffklappen 5-7

Änderungen: Maßstab: Tag: Angefertigt: Geprüft: Gesehen: Zeichn.-Nr.   Posee
FuA III. 124

Top and lower left: **Two views of the BMW 801C installed in the Ju 288 V7.**

Top right: **Works drawing of a Jumo 222 ducted cowling with annular radiator and attachment points for the Jumo 222 in the Ju 288B-1.**

Above right: **The Jumo 222A/B beneath the engine cowling.**

Left, above and bottom: **Three-quarter front view of the Jumo 222A/B (above) and (below) the streamlined aerodynamic cowling through which the propeller blades were anchored.**

The cooling section of the Jumo 222 with segments for water and oil cooling.

For mounting the engine in the aircraft, two Elektron beams combined with steel struts were used. The whole was fixed with an elastic rubber base and attached to the wing structure by four spherical universal joints. In the event of an emergency landing on water, the engines could be blown off to prevent the aircraft from sinking rapidly due to the extra powerplant weight. Power from the Jumo 222 was taken by the four-bladed Junkers VS 7 airscrews of 4m (13ft 1⅛in) diameter. Unlike the BMW 801, which was among the majority of air-cooled radials, the Jumo 222 required a liquid (water/glycol) cooling system, built of light metal in the form of an annular cooling radiator. Cooling air exhaust was arranged in the form of annular split flaps. A further variant had a so-called *Tunnelnabe* (ducted hub). In contrast to a short annular radiator, it took the form of an annular hood moved far forward that revolved together with the airscrews. An auxiliary cooling effect was achieved by means of special coverings in the roots of the propeller blading.

The origin of this unlucky engine design dates back to 1937, when Dipl.-Ing. Ferdinand Brandner* was assigned the task of developing a 24-cylinder motor. Following a two-year period of development and manufacture, the first prototype was run on the engine test-bed on 24th April 1939. To reach series-production maturity, however, several hurdles had to be overcome – obstacles which finally caused the project to founder. To cite Ferdinand Brandner:

'The tragedy of this engine development lay in the continual demands for performance increases that came from the airframe development side, which because of continually increasing weight excesses, could not attain the calculated flying performance. The Jumo 222 was thus developed to death.'

*For further details, see *Ein Leben zwischen Fronten (A Life Between Fronts):* Ferdinand Brandner; Weser-mühl Verlag, München/Wels, 1973, p.68 ff – Translator.

In its basic layout the Jumo 222 consisted of a 24-cylinder engine whose cylinders were arranged radially in four rows each of 6 cylinders – a configuration that combined the in-line with the radial type of construction. In the course of development, its cylinder volume was raised by increasing the bore from 135mm (5.31in) to 140mm (5.51in). The next step was to increase the stroke as well as the bore. The resulting differences in volume gave values of 46.6 litres (2,844in³), 49.8 litres (3,040in³) and 55.5 litres (3,387in³) respectively. Corresponding increases in the power of the Jumo 222 went from the initial 2,000hp at 2,900rpm to over 2,500hp at 3,000rpm and finally to the 3,000hp mark. The Jumo 222E/F, for example, was a high-altitude engine. The last projected step envisaged was a 36-cylinder variant with a 70-litre (4,273in³) displacement and a performance capability of up to 5,000hp (in the Jumo 225). The V-model of the Jumo 222G, 36 cylinders, 69.6 litres (4,260in³), achieved only 3,000hp.

Significant events in the development of the Jumo 222 according to Ferdinand Brandner's documents were:

- First test-run on 24th April 1939
- Confirmed attainment of 2,000hp in March 1940
- Removal of the Jumo 222 from large-scale production on 24th December 1941
- Confirmed 3,000hp achieved on 4th June 1942
- RLM again considers Jumo 222 in series production planning, August 1942
- According to *Bauprogramm* (Construction Programme) 35A of 11th February 1942, manufacture was to begin in Prague in October 1944. Until September 1945, a production total of 1,500 engines was planned.
- According to Ferdinand Brandner, 20 engines were available for the Fw 191 in 1943/44, but for reasons already described were not produced in series. Thus Heinkel received the Jumo 222A/B for the He 219.
- In summer 1944, design data for the Jumo 222 were sold to Japan. In January 1945, Brandner was scheduled to accompany the design and manufacturing drawings by submarine to Japan, but he remained in Germany.
- In January 1945, the Jumo 222 received highest priority as the sole engine capable of producing up to 3,000hp at 3,100rpm (Jumo 222C/D). It was almost identical to the 2,950hp DB 610 whose disadvantageous coupled layout caused higher drag that led to speed losses.

Daimler-Benz DB 606: The DB 606 was a high-power propulsion unit designed and produced within a relatively short time – a path that had also been followed by Allison in the USA when developing the V-1710 (installed in the Lockheed P-38) into the V-3420. The numbers here refer to the cylinder capacity in cubic inches. The development of the DB 610, however, was driven primarily by the need to remedy the lack of a suitable high-performance powerplant. Development of the DB 606 dated back to the He 119 whose notable maximum speed of 620km/h (385mph) was attained with this engine.

In the course of the Ju 288 programme, this coupled unit using 87 octane B4 fuel was installed in the Ju 288 V11, V13, V101 and V102 prototypes.

This 24-cylinder coupled engine consisted of two DB 601E units positioned side by side and inclined at 44° to each other, driving four-bladed propellers via a common driveshaft. The designation DB 606A/B signified that the propellers rotated to the right and left respectively. Total volume of the 24 cylinders of 154mm (6.06in) bore and 160mm (6.3in) stroke was 67.8 litres (4,138in³) and, in terms of power, developed 2,700hp at take-off and 2,400hp at climb and combat power. Rated altitude of the DB 610A/B was 4,900m (16,075ft), and for the DB 606C/D was 5,600m (17,965ft). Its considerable installation dimensions of 1,630mm (64⅛in) width, 1,060mm (41¾in) height and 2,082mm (82in) length had to be contained in a cowling of impressive size. As seen in the accompanying photograph, the radiator was built in the form of annular segments just behind the cowling air-intake lip. In terms of dry weight, its 1,400kg (3,086 lb) was 300kg (661 lb) more than the Jumo 222.

Engine fires in the DB 606 and DB 610 were due to several causes. For centre of gravity reasons, the powerplant was installed close to the wing main spar so the conduits involved using right-angled bends. Added to that, the cooling effect of the oil became less effective and which led to overheating problems, resulting in piston destruction. Conrod cracks and crankcase punctures occurred, often damaging the gearbox situated between the coupled engines.

Minor leaks, inadequate cooling air circulation and the close-fitting cowling in this region often had disastrous consequences. The oil came into contact with the centrally placed exhaust stacks and ignited. Furthermore, the exhaust-gas outlets were located in the vicinity of the undercarriage. Even small quantities of hydraulic fluid could therefore ignite on contact with the hot exhaust gases.

Daimler-Benz DB 610: As in the case of the DB 606, the DB 610 was also a coupled engine (based on the DB 605) in which a part could be disengaged if the need arose – a feature it shared with the DB 606. In principle, it functioned in a similar manner to the DB 606, having two one-stage superchargers and inertia starters. The DB 606A/B installed in the Ju 288 consisted of two 12-cylinder DB 605A motors that were likewise canted at 44° to each other. Compared to the DB 601, the DB 605 had a greater cylinder capacity and correspondingly higher power. Its 24 cylinders each of 154mm bore and 16mm stroke gave a total volume of 71.4 litres (4,360in³). With its dimensions of 1,632mm (64¼in) width, 1,057mm (41⅝in) height and 2,082mm (82in) length, it corresponded closely to the DB 606, but had a maximum dry weight of 1,570kg (3,461 lb). Because of their different gearing, the two coupled powerplants (A/B versions) had an individual weight difference of 40kg (88 lb).

The DB 610 engine was installed in the Ju 288 V103, V105, V106, V107 and V108 prototypes. Contradictory statements have appeared in various publications concerning the V102 powerplant. Some mention the DB 606, whilst others specify the DB 610. Exactly which of these units was actually installed cannot be established with certainty. It is possible that the DB 610 was fitted to the V102 at a later stage.

Installed in the Ju 288, the DB 610 turned out to be reliable. Although of high power, like the DB 606, it also had an inherent disadvantage in its design concept which resulted in a significant increase in frontal area and hence drag. The aerodynamic characteristics were therefore adversely affected, with a consequent reduction in the aircraft's maximum speed and a higher fuel consumption. This had to be evened out by carrying an increased quantity of 87 octane B4 fuel.

The Daimler-Benz DB 606 coupled engine.

Frontal view of the DB 606 cowling, showing the radiator segments near the cowling lip.

Works drawing of the DB 606A/B with table of power, rpm and sfc at various altitudes and power settings. The problems in connection with its installation in the He 177 were undoubtedly self-made. It was not the design of the powerplant itself but its faulty method of installation in the aircraft.

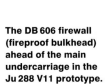

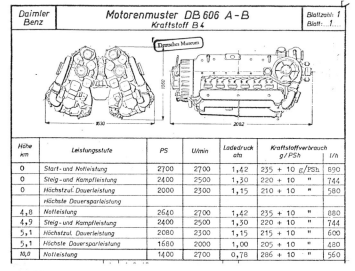

Daimler Benz	Motorenmuster DB 606 A - B Kraftstoff B 4				Blattzahl: 1 Blatt: 1	
Höhe km	Leistungsstufe	PS	U/min	Ladedruck ata	Kraftstoffverbrauch g/PSh	l/h
0	Start- und Notleistung	2700	2700	1,42	235 + 10 g/PSh	890
0	Steig- und Kampfleistung	2400	2500	1,30	220 + 10 "	744
0	Höchstzul. Dauerleistung	2000	2300	1,15	210 + 10 "	580
	Höchste Dauersparleistung					
4,8	Notleistung	2640	2700	1,42	235 + 10 "	880
4,9	Steig- und Kampfleistung	2400	2500	1,30	220 + 10 "	744
5,1	Höchstzul. Dauerleistung	2080	2300	1,15	215 + 10 "	600
5,1	Höchste Dauersparleistung	1680	2000	1,00	205 + 10 "	480
10,0	Notleistung	1400	2700	0,78	286 + 10 "	560

The DB 606 firewall (fireproof bulkhead) ahead of the main undercarriage in the Ju 288 V11 prototype.

8/39

S
J.46 63

288/36

S
J.46 630

288/40

S
J.46 63

V6

S
J.46 629

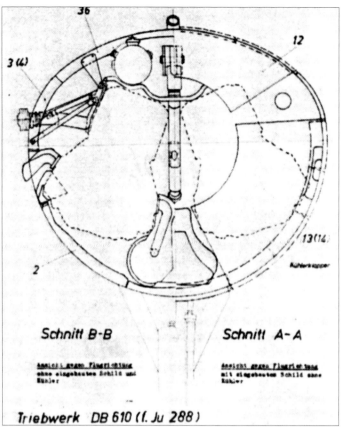

Schnitt B-B

Ansicht gegen Flugrichtung
ohne eingebautes Schild und
Kühler

Schnitt A-A

Ansicht gegen Flugrichtung
mit eingebautem Schild ohne
Kühler

Triebwerk DB 610 (f. Ju 288)

Opposite page:

Top left: **The coupled DB 610. Note the long drive shaft.**

Centre left: **Head-on view of the DB 610 cowling with its annular arrangement of radiator segments. Note the similarity to the DB 606 illustration.**

Bottom left: : **Rear perspective of the light-metal radiator segments and four of the six port side exhaust stacks.**

Top right: **The starboard supercharger and ducting on the DB 610 photographed on display in the aircraft park in Schleißheim.**

Centre right: **This rear view shows the complex network of wiring and conduits above and to the right of the powerplant.**

Bottom right: **A segment of the cowling with radiator gills.**

This page:

Top left: **Extended view of the uncowled DB 610 port side supercharger behind the six exhaust stacks.**

Above: **Cross-sectional front view of the DB 610 in the Ju 288.**

Below: **Cross-sectional side view of the DB 610A/B with radiator gills at A-B.**

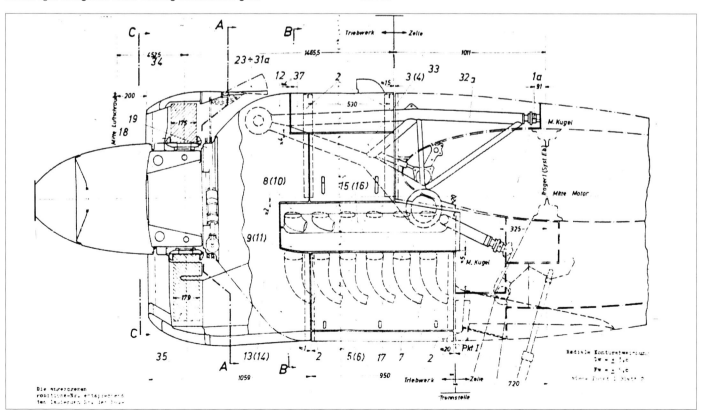

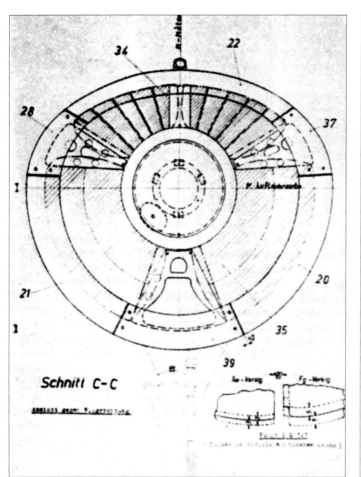

Schnitt C-C

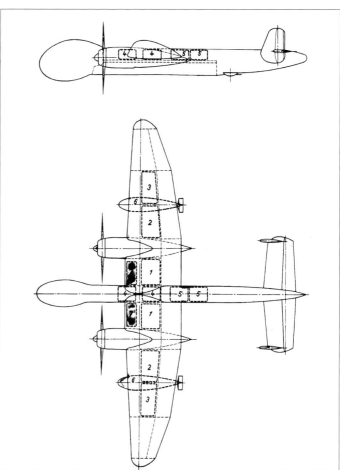

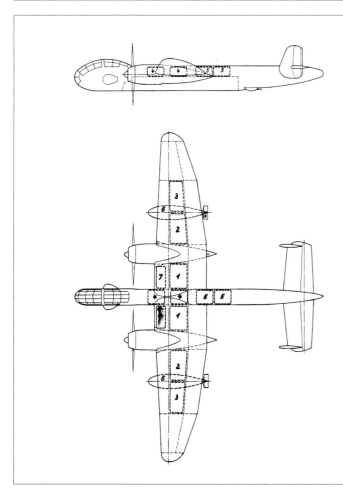

Ju 288 A   Kraft-und Schmierstoffbehälter.

Normale Kraftstoffbehälter:

Flügel:	①	2 x 720 l.	= 1440 l.
	②	2 x 660 l.	= 1320 l.
	③	2 x 400 l.	= 800 l.
			3560 l.
Rumpf:	④ + ⑤	4 x 450 l.	= 1800 l.
	Gesamt		**= 5360 l.**

Zusätzliche Kraftstoffbehälter:
auswechselbar gegen Bombenlasten
und abwerfbar.

Aussenbehälter:	⑥	2 x 900 l.	= 1800 l.

Tanks ④ **sind Entnahmebehälter.**
Tanks ① + ② **besitzen Schnellablass.**
Größte Kraftstoffmenge   **7160 l.**

Schmierstoffbehälter:

Flügelnase:	●	2 x 230 l.	= 460 l.

96933

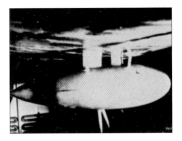

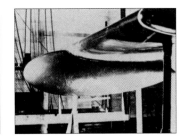

Opposite page:

Top left: **A further detail of the DB 610A/B annular radiator design.**

Top right: **Ju 288B wing and fuselage fuel tanks (1 to 5), drop-tanks (6) and shaded lubricant tanks ahead of the wing centre-section main spar.**

Bottom: **Arrangement and capacities of the fuel and lubricant tanks in the Ju 288A.**

This page:

Top row: **Various configurations evolved for the underwing auxiliary drop-tanks.**

Above: **Head-on view of the Ju 288 (2 x BMW 801s) with its twin mainwheels of 5.5m (18ft 0½in) track.**

Fuel System

As already mentioned, the fuel and lubricant oil tanks were housed in the wings and fuselage in the Ju 288 and consisted of:

- 4 x 450 litres in protected bag-tanks in the upper fuselage between frames 2-3, 4-5, 6-7 and 7-8. In the Ju 288 V6 drawing, there were only three fuselage fuel tanks.
- 2 x 720-litre bag-tanks in the wing centre section
- 2 x 660-litre bag-tanks in the nearer wing outer sections
- 2 x 400-litre bag-tanks in the further wing outer sections
- 2 x 900-litre drop-tanks on stations beneath the outer wings

The aircraft therefore held a total of 7,160 litres, comprising 5,360 litres internally and 1,800 litres externally, plus 2 x 230-litre lubricant oil tanks in the wing centre section. Total fuel in the Ju 288A was identical to the Ju 288B. Fuel capacity for the Ju 288C was identical to its pre-

decessors, but was planned to be increased from 7,160 litres to a total of 8,650 litres which included the 2 x 900-litre drop-tanks.

Undercarriage

These components of the Ju 288 were made up of the twin retractable mainwheels and single retractable tailwheel. On the Ju 288A, the twin mainwheels each measured 935 x 345mm (36.8 x 13.6in) and had hydraulically operated double servo-brakes. Between the wheel pairs was a compressed-air leg combined with auxiliary oil damping, each undercarriage unit with its supporting fork and compression/extension struts retracting rearwards hydraulically into the wing centre section as shown in a *contemporary* graphical illustration (p.42). For the Ju 288B and C, mainwheel dimensions were increased to 1,015 x 380mm (40 x 15in); mainwheel track was 5.5m (18ft 0½in). The tailwheel, measuring 630 x 220mm (24.8 x 8.7in), retracted rearwards between fuselage frames 13 and 15 in all versions of the aircraft.

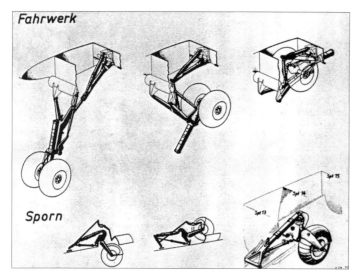

Fahrwerk

Sporn

Spt 15
Spt 14
Spt 13

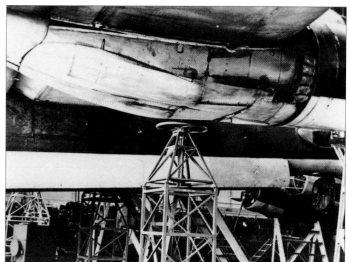

Military Equipment

The armament of the Ju 288 has already been extensively covered, so only a few details are added here, expanded with the aid of drawings and photographs. Of interest is a handbook extract on the FA-15 remote drive which, in shortened form, is provided with the technical description of the Ju 388. There now follows some technical data on the various types of weapons and bombs.

Opposite page:

Top left: **Retraction sequence of the mainwheels (upper) and tailwheel (lower).**

Centre left: **The Ju 288 mainwheels of 935 x 345mm, in the locked-down mode**

Bottom left: **The mainwheels during the retraction sequence.**

Top right: **The mainwheels are now fully retracted.**

Centre right: **Inside the tailwheel bay.**

Bottom right: **The 630 x 220mm tailwheel with wheel fork, mudguard and swivel hinge.**

This page:

Top right: **Location of the starboard blister and ventral periscope sight.**

Below: **Close-up of the dorsal periscope behind the cockpit.**

Bottom right: **In the foreground is the steering mechanism for the remote-controlled weapon installation.**

Bottom left: **The B-Stand aft of the cockpit and periscope.**

J.30451.

J.30453.

J.42760

J.42763

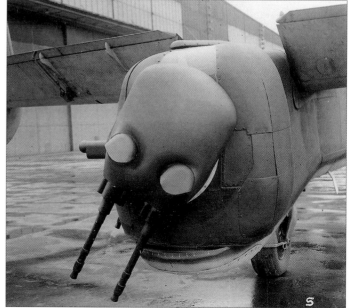

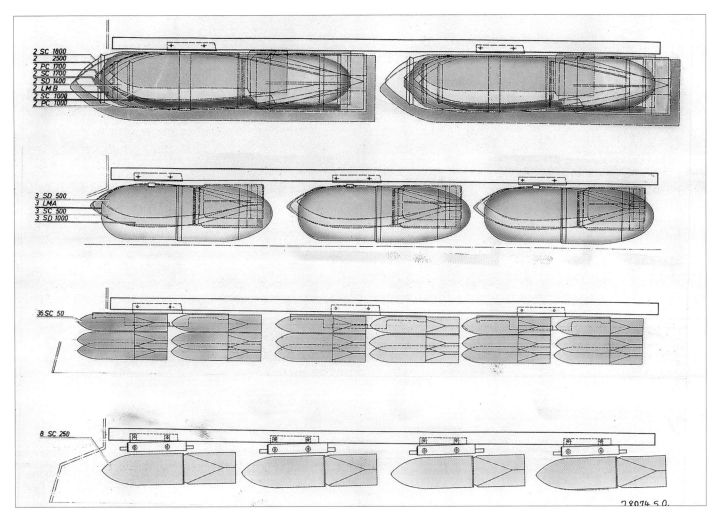

Opposite page:

Top left: **Mock-up of the ventral C2-Stand.**

Centre left: **Ammunition feed-belts in the mock-up C2-Stand.**

Top right: **This type of manned H-Stand (tail barbette) did not meet with RLM approval.**

Centre right: **The mock-up weapons at their maximum upward angle.**

Bottom left: **The rather cramped manned H-Stand with its covering panel removed.**

Bottom right: **Mock-up of another type of tail barbette directed downwards.**

This page:

Top: **Ju 288 bombload variation possibilities without modifications to the bomb bay.**

Ju 288 Bomb Data Comparison

Qty	Weapon	Type	Diameter mm (in)		Length mm (in)		Weight kg (lb)		Tolerance [+/-], kg (lb)		Explosive kg (lb)	
36 x	SC 50	M	200	(7.87)	1,100	(43.31)	50	(110)	4	(8.8)	25	(55)
8 x	SC 250	M	368	(14.49)	1,640	(64.57)	250	(551)	12	(26.5)	125	(276)
3 x	SC 500	M	470	(18.50)	2,010	(79.13)	500	(1,102)	20	(44.9)	260	(573)
2 x	SC 1000	M	654	(25.75)	2,580	(101.6)	1,027	(2,264)	34	(75)	560	(1,236)
2 x	SC 1800*	M	660	(25.98)	3,500	(137.8)	1,832	(4,039)	65	(143)	1,000	(2,205)
2 x	SC 2500*	G	829	(32.64)	3,895	(153.3)	2,500	(5,512)	70	(154)	1,700	(3,748)
3 x	SD 500	S	396	(15.59)	2,007	(79.02)	480	(1,058)	23	(50.7)	90	(198)
3 x	SD 1000	S	500	(19.69)	2,100	(82.68)	1,000	(2,205)	55	(121)	160	(353)
2 x	SD 1400	S	562	(22.13)	2,836	(111.7)	1,400	(3,086)	-		300	(661)
2 x	PC 1000	P	500	(19.69)	2,100	(82.68)	988	(2,178)	50	(110)	152	(335)
3 x	LM A	F	646	(25.43)	2,660	(104.7)	650	(1,433)	-		300	(661)
2 x	LM B	F	660	(25.98)	3,040	(119.7)	1,000	(2,205)	50	(110)	680	(1,499)

SC = Thin-walled bomb with c.50% weight of high-explosive; general-purpose bomb.
SD = Thick-walled bomb with c.30% weight of explosive, high fragmentation effect; multi-purpose targets.
PC = Thick-walled high-penetration steel-cased bomb with c.20% weight of h.e; used for ships and fortifications.
LM = Luftmine. Air-dropped sea-mine.
M = Minenbombe. Standard bomb. Explosive content varied: Trialen, Amatol, Ammonal, etc.
G = Großladungsbombe. High % of explosive in total weight. Strong pressure-wave destructive effect.
S = Splitterbombe. Fragmentation bomb, multi-purpose use against high-rise buildings, industrial complexes, etc.
P = Panzersprengbombe. Armour-piercing h.e. bomb; used against concrete, bridges, ships, underground targets.
F = Flugzeugmine. (lit. Aircraft-carried mine).
* = at overload condition. Normal bombload was 3,000kg (6,614 lb).

Top: **Looking down the Ju 288 bomb bay.**

Above: **Loading such heavy 'hummers' was no problem.**

Right: **Further developments of the Ju 288 with (upper) various armament alternatives and (lower) powered by 2 x 2,200hp BMW 802 radials.**

Ju 288 Armament Data Comparison

	Mauser MG 81	Rh.-Borsig MG 131	Rh.-Borsig MG 151/15	Rh.-Borsig MG 151/20
Calibre, mm (in)	7.92 (0.31)	13 (0.51)	15 (0.59)	20 (0.79)
Rate of fire, rds/min	1,600	930	660-700*	630-780*
Initial velocity, m/sec (ft/sec)	705-875 2,313-1,871	710-750* 2,321-2,461	850-1,030* 2,789-3,346	695-785* 2,280-2,575
Barrel length, mm (in)	475 (18.70)	546 (21.50)	1,254 (49.37)	1,104 (43.46)
Weapon length, mm (in)	915 (36.03)	1,168 (45.98)	1,916 (75.43)	1,766 (69.53)
Weapon width, mm (in)	114 (4.49)	233 (9.17)	190 (7.48)	190 (7.48)
Weapon height, mm (in)	183 (7.20)	123 (4.84)	195 (7.68)	195 (7.68)
Weapon weight, kg (lb)	6.5 (14.33)	19.7 (43.43)	42.7 (94.14)	42.5 (93.70)
Ammo belt weight (100 rds), kg (lb)	7.80 (17.20)	8.36 (18.43)	16.82 (37.08)	19.90 (43.87)
Belt length (100 rds), mm (in)	- -	2385 (93.90)	3310 (130.03)	3310 (130.03)
Projectile weight fired/sec, kg (lb)	0.308 (0.68)	0.527 (1.16)	0.665 (1.47)	1.080 (2.38)
Type of ammunition	SmK	Spr.Gr.	Spr.Gr.	M.Gr.

* According to type of ammunition; SmK = steel-core pointed-nose shell; Spr.Gr. = high-explosive incendiary shell; M.Gr. = high-explosive normal shell; Rh.-Borsig = Rheinmetall-Borsig.

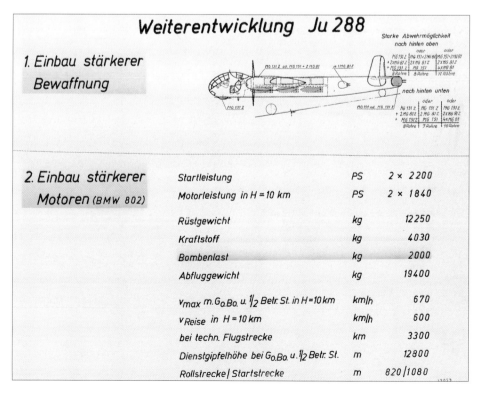

Junkers Ju 288-Series Data Comparison

	Ju 288A	Ju 288B	Ju 288C
Powerplants			
Designation	2 x Jumo 222A/B	2 x Jumo 222E/F	2 x DB 610A/B*
Take-off power (each)	2,000hp at 2,900rpm	2,500hp at 3,000rpm	2,950hp at 2,800rpm
Combat power (each)	1,980hp at 2,900rpm	1,750hp at 2,900rpm	2,710hp at 2,800rpm
Max. continuous power	1,800hp at 2,700rpm	-	2,150hp at 2,300rpm
Rated altitude, m (ft)	6,400 (21,000)	9,400 (30,840)	5,800 (19,030)
Supercharger	2-speed	2-stage	2 x 1-stage
Dimensions			
Overall span	22.00m (72' 2⅛")	22.60m (74' 1¾")	22.60m (74' 1¾")†
Centre-section span	6.67m (21' 10⅝")	6.67m (21' 10⅝")	6.67m (21' 10⅝")
Outer wing span (x 2)	7.665m (25' 1¾")	7.965m (26' 1⅝")	7.965m (26' 1⅝")
Overall length	16.60m (54' 5.5")	18.10m (59' 4⅝")	18.15m (59' 6½")
Height	4.60m (15' 1⅛")	5.00m (16' 4⅞")	5.00m (16' 4⅞")
Wing area, m² (ft²)	60.00 (645.82)	64.70 (696.41)	64.70 (696.41)
Aspect ratio	8.10	7.90	7.90
Wing power loading, hp/m² (hp/ft²)	66.7 (6.2)	77.3 (7.2)	91.2 (8.5)
Power/weight ratio, kg/hp (lb/hp)	4.325 (9.53)	4.240 (9.35)	3.695 (8.15)
Weights			
Equipped weight, kg (lb)	11,000kg (24,251 lb)	13,600 (29,983)	13,000 (28,660)
Payload (with 3T bombs), kg (lb)	6,800 (13,889)	7,600 (16,755)	8,800 (19,400)
Take-off weight, kg (lb)	17,300 (38,140)	21,200 (46,738)	21,800 (48,060)
Payload/take-off weight	36.4%	35.8%	40.4%
Performance			
Maximum speed	645km/h at 6,000m (401mph at 19,685ft)	625km/h at 6,000m (388mph at 19,685ft)	655km/h at 6,800m (407mph at 22,310ft)
Cruising speed	565km/h at 6,000m (351mph at 19,685ft)	545km/h at 8,000m (339mph at 26,250ft)	520km/h at 6,800m (323mph at 22,310ft)
Initial climb rate, m/sec (ft/min)	7.1 (1,398)	6.2 (1,220)	8.2 (1,614)
Times to height, min			
to 4,000m (13,120ft)	-	10	-
to 6,000m (19,685ft)	-	16.5	-
to 8,000m (26,250ft)	-	27	-
Range, km (miles)	3,850 (2,392)	3,600 (2,237)	3,800 (2,361)
Service ceiling, m (ft)	10,300 (33,790)	9,400 (30,840)	10,390 (34,090)
Endurance, hours	7.00	6.60	5.40
Take-off run, m (ft)	1,050 (3,445)	1,100 (3,609)	1,200 (3,937)
Landing run, m (ft)	1,000 (3,281)	1,000 (3,281)	1,000 (3,281)
Landing speed, km/h (mph)	180 (112)	175 (109)	175 (109)
Armament per Datasheet			
(with number of rounds)			
A-Stand	2 x MG 81 (1,400)	1 x MG 131Z (2,000)	1 x MG 131Z (2,000)
B-Stand	1x MG 131Z (2,000)	1 x MG 131Z (2,000)	1 x MG 131Z (2,000)
C-Stand	1x MG 131Z (2,000)	-	-
D-Stand	-	-	1 x MG 131Z (2,000)
H-Stand	1x MG 151 (700)	1 x MG 151 (700)	1 x MG 151 (700)
Maximum bombload, kg (lb)	3,000 (6,614)	3,000 (6,614)	3,000 (6,614)
(composition as per previous table)			
Crew	three	four	four

*DB 610A/B maximum power 3,100hp at 2,000m (6,560ft).

† Span also quoted as 22.99m (75ft 5⅛in) and wing area 65.00m² (699.64ft²).

Chapter Five

Enthusiastic Plans

Ju 288 Production Planning

During the development and construction phase of the Ju 288, there was a greater emphasis on even closer co-operation between the design and manufacturing sectors. A production-oriented design meant that fewer specialists and other personnel were needed during manufacture to achieve a higher production rate, the aim having been to unify all phases as much as possible. This type of organisation was therefore of a completely different structure from the Ju 88 programme, for example. New manufacturing techniques were being planned; the spot-welding method to accelerate production was undergoing testing, for which research was being conducted into optical methods in relation to the then still critical welding of light metal. From now on, spot-welding was to replace the traditional riveted joints in all possible areas of construction. For this purpose, I.G. Farben at the Bitterfeld works was to be equipped with a 30,000 tonne forging press with which, for example, the 10m (32.8ft) long main spar box could be fabricated in one piece, and would have been the world's largest press. A further criterion to accelerate production was the conveyor-belt system of manufacture. The so-called 'rail-track' production method naturally called for a completely different set of manufacturing techniques.

The plan to enable various groups of structural parts to be manufactured by several sub-contracting firms had already encountered significant problems with the Ju 88. For example, a large-scale attempt carried out in 1940 showed that four out of ten components checked had to be improved in order to make them fit exactly in an aircraft having similar variants. Precise fitting of the parts delivered was a logical prerequisite of a functioning factory assembly line. The so-called *Lochbauweise* manufacturing method was therefore introduced which, with the aid of moulds, templates and the copy-press method, considerably improved accuracy and precision in the manufacture of the various parts. This new method was to largely replace the traditional one consisting of drawings, jigs and measurement checks. For the Ju 288, a total of 32 manufacturing groups of components were envisaged, excluding powerplant and equipment parts.

Junkers Director Heinrich Koppenberg saw the Ju 288 as the ideal starting point for his expansion plans. In 1940, he strongly maintained that in a few generations there would only be Junkers aircraft – an opinion that any objective observer would have considered laughable.

The following table shows the manufacture of medium bombers in the years 1942 to 1944:

Prod'n Year	Junkers Ju 88 - 388	Heinkel He 111	Dornier Do 217	Annual Total
1942	3,094*	1,337	721	5,152
1943	3,530*	1,405	711	5,646
1944	4,009	759	-	4,768
Totals	**10,633**	**3,501**	**1,432**	**15,566**

*Without Ju 388. Do 217 production was terminated in the last quarter of 1943.

As these figures indicate, between the 1st quarter of 1942 and the 4th quarter of 1944, 10,633 examples of the Ju 88, Ju 188, Ju 288 and Ju 388 left the final assembly lines. From the 1st quarter of 1942 to the 3rd quarter of 1944, 3,501 He 111s were manufactured. Production of this aircraft that had flown in the Spanish Civil War stopped in September 1944. In May 1944 the He 177 and the legendary Ju 87 'Stuka', the weapon of the *Blitzkrieg* (lightning war) era, had already shared the same fate, when the last 21 examples were completed. In comparison, only 1,432 examples of various versions of the Do 217 left the production lines between the 1st quarter of 1942 and the end of production in the 4th quarter of 1943, when the last airframe left the final assembly line. With regard to the air situation over the Third Reich, fighters now had the highest priority because of the need to protect production centres from the ever-increasing enemy bombardment which resulted in the rapid decentralisation of production. This concept of Armaments Minister Albert Speer and his deputy, Department Head Dipl.-Ing. Karl-Otto Saur developed swiftly, and production totals soon reached an all-time high. However, these figures were attained at the expense of forced labourers and concentration camp inmates. Numerous documents bear witness to the tragedy of this period. Largely forgotten in this connection, however, is that a similar fate befell thousands of German prisoners of war and civilians deported post-war to the Soviet Union. This is not tainted propaganda but an undeniable fact of history.

At the time when all these events became brutal reality, the RLM also decided finally to bury the Ju 288. The Junkers portion of the 'Bomber B' programme had been the most expensive of its development projects and also of the entire German aviation industry. As with the Ju 88 project, which also experienced innumerable problems, it had existed only for a short while as a grand plan of Heinrich Koppenberg.

From its very beginning during the pre-war era up to the completion of work on the Ju 288 towards the middle of 1944, the project swallowed up the then gigantic sum of 84 million Reichsmarks. As a comparison in the field of aircraft development, Hugo Junkers spent only about one-sixth of this sum between 1916 and 1929 (see chart on page 51).

Let us now consider the enthusiastic plans based on the following figures (which exclude the numbers of prototypes produced). Production planning began with a *Versuchsserie* (test series), the first aircraft of which was to have been completed in November 1940. One further example was to follow each month in March, April and May 1941, as well as three aircraft in December that year.

The pre-production *Nullserie* (zero series) aircraft, designated strangely enough as the A-1 and B-1, were to enter production in January 1942. Completion was scheduled as follows:

Year	Month	Ju 288A-1	Ju 288B-1
1942	Jan	1	1
1942	Feb	2	1
1942	Mar	3	1
1942	Apr	4	0
1942	May	5	2
1942	June	5	1
1942	July	6	1
1942	Aug	6	0
1942	Sept	0	6
1942	Oct	0	5
1942	Nov	0	3
1942	Dec	0	2
Total:		**32**	**23**

In addition to the above totals, series production of 16 examples of the planned Ju 288B-3 was to have overlapped during the period August to

December 1942. According to plans, five other firms besides Junkers were to have participated in Ju 288B-3 production until December 1945. Distribution was to have been as follows:

Junkers

As mentioned above, the Junkers facilities were to have begun production of the Ju 288B-3 in August 1942. Until June 1942, the numbers of planned aircraft increased continually. Whereas during August and September 1941, one aircraft would be produced, the monthly completion rate rose to two in October, four in November and eight in December 1941. In January 1942, the monthly production rate was to rise to 15 aircraft per month. Taking into account the so-called 'learning curve' representing a measure of the learning success of the workers and the continual optimisation of production processes based on experience gained, production plans called for 25 aircraft in February, 40 in March, 50 in April and even 60 in May 1943. From June 1943 until December 1945, the required number of aircraft remained constant at 80 per month, that is 31 months x 80 = 2,480 aircraft. The grand total of Ju 288 production planned at Junkers was therefore 2,783 aircraft.

Successive installation and verification sequences in manufacture of the Ju 288 high-altitude pressurised cabin for the V6 prototype.

Licence Manufacturers

According to production planning, five further firms were to have become involved in the manufacturing process. Here, the required numbers of aircraft varied considerably, with the exception of the two last-named firms.

The licence manufacturers comprised the firms of Arado, ATG, Dornier, Heinkel, Henschel and Siebel. The available documents unfortunately do not make it possible to identify the firms individually in the following list of licence manufacturers.

Licence Firm No 1

At this firm, production was to have begun in February 1943. The number of aircraft planned to leave the final assembly lines were: February: 1, March: 2, April: 4, May: 5, June: 12, July: 20, August: 30 and September: 40. From October 1943 until December 1945 inclusive, the figure remained constant at 45 per month, giving a Ju 288B-3 production total of 1,329 aircraft.

Licence Firm No 2

Here, manufacture was to begin in February 1943, and corresponding production quantities were: February: 1, March: 2, April: 4 and May: 8, expanding in succeeding months to June: 15, July: 25, August: 40 and September: 50. From October 1943 until December 1945, Ju 288B-3 production remained constant at 60 aircraft per month, giving a total of 1,765 aircraft.

Licence Firm No 3

Production activity was planned to start here in March 1943, with these monthly figures: March: 1, April: 2, May: 4, June: 7 and July: 12. From then on, the figures were to increase to August: 20, September: 30 and October: 40, to a maximum of 50 from November – a monthly figure which was to extend until December 1945. The Ju 288B-3 production total for this firm was thus 1,416 aircraft.

Licence Firms Nos 4 and 5

In accordance with directives, both firms were to have started production in April 1943, with identical numbers being produced by each firm per month. In the initial phase, from April to September, numbers to be turned out monthly were: April: 1, May: 2, June: 4, July: 7, August: 12 and September: 20. In both firms, 25 Ju 288B-3s were to be produced monthly between October 1943 and December 1945. Each firm would therefore have had some 50% of the capacity of Licence Firm No 3. This came to 721 aircraft per firm, or 1,442 aircraft in total.

The sum of all production numbers gives a total of 8,697 aircraft for the Ju 288A-1, B-1 and B-3, to which must be added the ten test prototypes. Excluded from these figures is a detailed listing of the Ju 288C, a version that was to have been powered by the so-called 'fall-back' or alternative engines. Since the Jumo 222 was not avail-

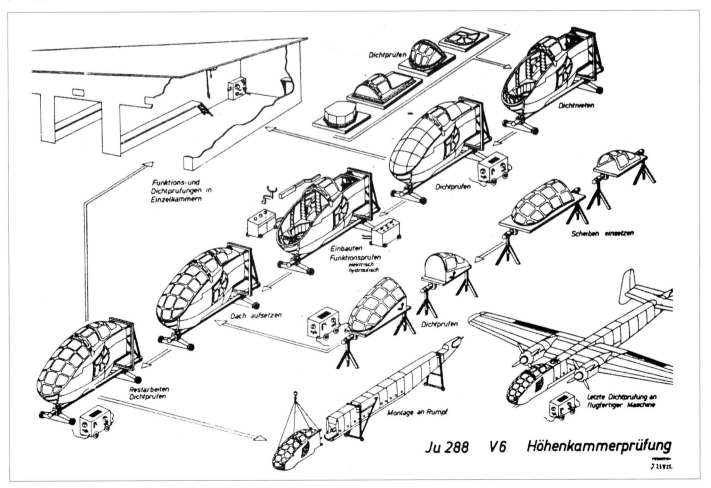

Ju 288 V6 Höhenkammerprüfung

Planned Ju 288 Monthly Production

Production Year	Month	Prototypes Ju 288	Nullserie Ju 288A-1	Nullserie Ju 288B-1	Großserie Ju 288B-3	Combined Total
1940	Nov	1	-	-	-	
1940	Dec	1	-	-	-	
1941	Jan	1	-	-	-	
1941	Feb	1	-	-	-	
1941	Mar	1	-	-	-	
1941	Apr	1	-	-	-	
1941	May	1	-	-	-	
1941	June	-	-	-	-	
1941	July	-	-	-	-	
1941	Aug	1	-	-	-	
1941	Sept	-	-	-	-	
1941	Oct	-	-	-	-	
1941	Nov	-	-	-	-	
1941	Dec	3	-	-	-	
1942	Jan	1	1*	1*	-	3
1942	Feb	1	2*	1*	-	4
1942	Mar	-	3†	1†	-	4
1942	Apr	-	4†	-	-	4
1942	May	-	5†	1†	-	6
1942	June	-	5†	1†	-	6
1942	July	-	6†	1†	-	7
1942	Aug	-	6†	-	1	7
1942	Sept	-	-	6†	1	7
1942	Oct	-	-	5†	2	7
1942	Nov	-	-	3†	4	7
1942	Dec	-	-	2	8	10
1943	Jan	-	-	-	15	
1943	Feb	-	-	-	27	
1943	Mar	-	-	-	45	
1943	Apr	-	-	-	62	
1943	May	-	-	-	83	
1943	June	-	-	-	122	
1943	July	-	-	-	151	
1943	Aug	-	-	-	194	
1943	Sept	-	-	-	240	
1943	Oct	-	-	-	275	
1943	Nov	-	-	-	285	
1943	Dec	-	-	-	285	
1944	Jan–Dec	-	-		285 each month	
1945	Jan–Dec	-	-		285 each month	
Total:		10	32	22	8,640	

* Test aircraft. †For the Ju 288, the pre-production 0-series was designated A-1 and B-1.

able, it had been decided to use the DB 61 if necessary. This would have required several modifications that would have delayed the project even further. Only prototypes of this variant of the Ju 288 left the assembly lines.

The Reality

From the original optimistic production figures, only a small number of prototypes were actually built. These, just 22 in all, were the meagre result of immense efforts expended on design, planning and manufacture, all of which involved horrendous sums that exceeded the expenditure of any previous German aircraft development project. So the Ju 288 met the same fate as the other 'Bomber B' competitors. Seen as a whole, the entire programme involving Arado, Dornier, Focke-Wulf, Henschel and Junkers achieved little, except for the fact that three of the firms were able to advance their designs up to prototype status.

In view of the effort involved, it was a poor outcome, caused by changes in priorities and the RLM decisions that resulted from them. The huge financial outlay which the firms wasted was by no means the most important consideration in wartime. A more weighty factor was time, which became increasingly pressing for both the manufacturers and the Luftwaffe. Admittedly, extremely valuable experience had been gained during the course of development of the Ju 288, but the flying formations urgently needed new bombers with improved performance capabilities and this requirement remained unfulfilled. The flying units therefore had to go into battle with what was available to them. Hence the Ju 88, He 111, He 177 and Do 217 had to serve continuously at the Front.

Changes in Priorities

Following the demise of the 'Bomber B', various manufacturers were busy with numerous other projects, among them the Ju 288. With this conglomeration of various Junkers designs, the expectations were just as high as for the 'Bomber B'. The costs and results of this work are covered in a separate chapter.

So what could have become available following the abandonment of the Ju 288 programme? On the one hand, there were the efficient versions of the Ju 88 and Ju 188. On the other, were Dornier and Heinkel's standard models with increased performance:
- the Ju 88S-1/S-2 with the BMW 801G, and the Ju 88S-3 with the Jumo 213A
- the Ju 188A-1/A-2/S-1 with the Jumo 213A
- the Do 217P with the DB 603S, and the Do 217R with the DB 603A
- the He 111R-1/R-2/R-3, each powered by the DB 603. Further proposals worked out in the meantime by Heinkel envisaged the use of the Jumo 213A and B as well as the Jumo 223 engine.

These powerplants had, or would have, undoubtedly improved the performance of the abovementioned aircraft significantly. Even so, these aircraft types were still not able to compete with the ever-rising standards being set by the performance advances made by the enemy. The aircrews therefore often suffered the consequences by paying with their lives.

Attention was now turned in the direction of the jet-propelled bomber. For a long time, consideration had been given to the idea of an armada of bomb-laden Me 262s or strategic jet bombers with which it was hoped to avenge the increasing destruction of German cities by the British and Americans. In the design offices of the aircraft firms, a veritable flood of such projects appeared, but only an extremely small number of these came to fruition. The overwhelming number of these bold and elegant designs remained a sort of engineers' 'occupational therapy'. Several thousands of man-hours were expended on these all-too-often unrealistic and impracticable projects. The innovations and know-how stemming from those designs that were grounded in hard reality were soon to be the fruits harvested by the victors of the war. The time had long since passed when they would be used for the benefit of Germany. At least the individuals working on countless such projects did not have to be drafted into frontline service, although this exemption could be cancelled at any time. This *Heldenklau* (literally, clawing of heroes) meant that many a highly qualified employee met his death at the frontline for a lost cause.

Besides the Me 262, the Ar 234 went into series production for the fast bomber role. This aircraft was certainly exceedingly fast, but in terms of range and projected bombload was not entirely convincing as it relied exclusively on new technology with all the associated teething troubles. Given sufficient time, the problems would undoubtedly have been overcome. But time was precisely the factor that was no longer available at this stage of the war. A satisfactory and speedily achievable solution would undoubtedly have been the Ju 388. In the fast bomber, reconnaissance and night-fighter role, the equally predestined Do 335

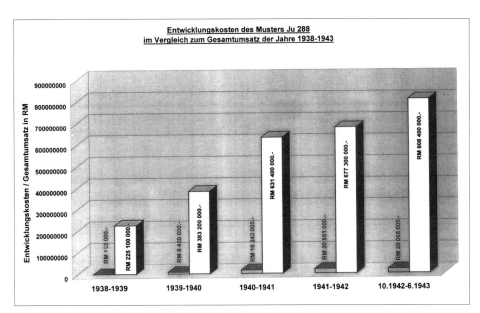

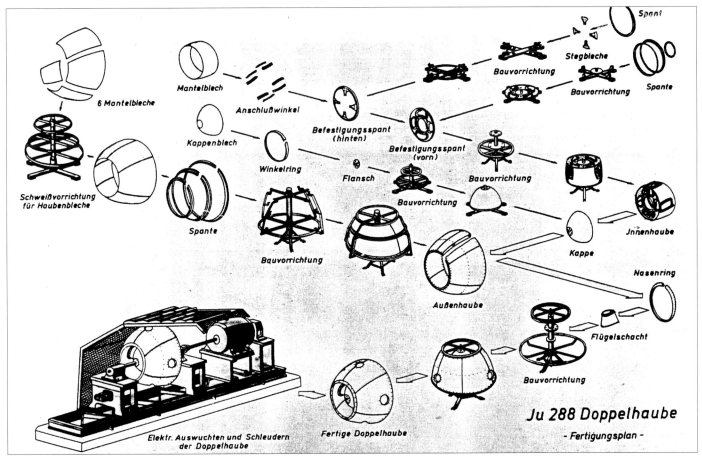

Top: **Ju 288 development costs in Reichsmarks in relation to total turnover of the Junkers-Werke for the period 1938 to 1943.**

Above: **Manufacturing sequences of the Ju 288 engine boss and intake cowling.**

should also be mentioned here. Even this, how-ever, did not go beyond the small series-pro-duction stage. All of the design proposals based on the Do 335 partly conceived with mixed (jet and airscrew) propulsion remained on the drawing board. A real opportunity for the

medium bomber, the night-fighter and recon-naissance units was presented by the Ju 388. However, forthcoming events in this case, too, permitted only a limited appearance of this promising aircraft.

New Goals
The need to forge a new and effective fight-ing weapon required contributions from other spheres of air armament activity, and Septem-ber 1944 serves as an example. In that month, 3,821 aircraft of various types were delivered. Predominant among these was the long-

neglected fighter production which now took priority, 3,670 of this number consisting of fight-ers, fighter-bombers and reconnaissance air-craft. The bomber arm received a mere 118 aircraft. This was because the complete disso-lution of the bomber wings had already begun and bomber units were being partly dissolved or transformed into KG(J) = Kampfgesch-wader (Jäger) or bomber wing (fighter) units. The remaining 33 aircraft consisted of trans-ports, ground-attack aircraft and flying boats. Of the brand-new Ar 234 and Ju 388, only 18 and 3 respectively were delivered.

51

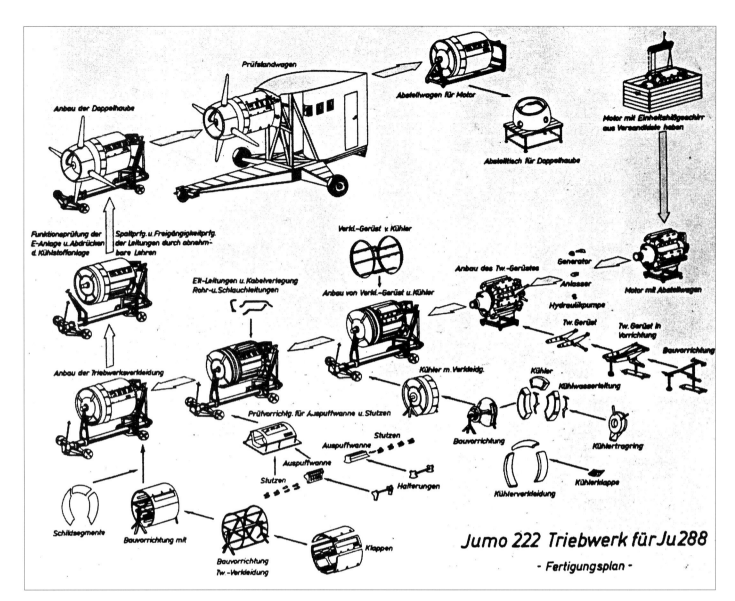

Jumo 222 Triebwerk für Ju 288
- Fertigungsplan -

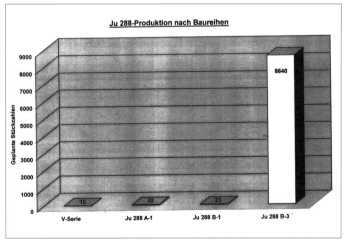

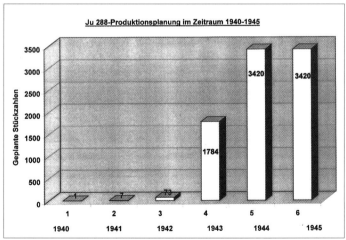

Top: **Manufacturing sequences of the Jumo 222 engine for the Ju 288.**

Above left: **Planned production totals of each of the Ju 288-Series.**

Above right: **Planned Ju 288 production by year.**

Chapter Six

The Favourite

The Path to the Ju 388

The Transitional Model – The Ju 88B

For the sake of completeness, the Ju 188 is mentioned here since to some extent it served as a stand-in following the demise of the Ju 288. It had its origins in the Ju 88B whose spherical glazed cockpit area presented a completely different appearance from that of the 'traditional' Ju 88 bomber. This area corresponded to that of the Ju 188, equipped with a fully glazed canopy offering the crew improved all-round vision, and more room. This model also had more powerful engines, the 1,560hp BMW 801MA 14-cylinder twin-row radial replacing the 1,420hp Jumo 211 in-line. According to data sheets, the Ju 88B-0 was initially intended to be powered by the Jumo 213, but due to engine delivery problems designers had to fall back on the BMW 801 as powerplant.

The most important differences between the Ju 88A and the Ju 88B in summary were:
- A much-improved full-view cockpit canopy instead of the stepped canopy
- Jumo 211F replaced with the BMW 801MA
- Revised armament consisting of 3 x MG 81Z in the Ju 88B-0, and 1 x MG 151, 3 x MG 17, 1 x MG 81 and 1 x MG 81Z in the Ju 88B-3 Zerstörer (heavy fighter)
- Improved aerodynamics giving higher speed.

The first aircraft in Ju 88B configuration was the V23 (D-ARYB) prototype. Bearing c/n 2001, it made its maiden flight on 19th June 1940. Flown by Flugkapitän Rupprecht Wendel, who also flew the V24 (D-ASGQ) for the first time on 30th July 1940. These were followed by examples of the Ju 88B-0 which left the final assembly lines in the summer of that year. The aircraft were subsequently used for service testing or were thoroughly tested by the manufacturer with various engine and armament installations. All of these aircraft formed the direct link to the Ju 188. Initially bearing prototype designations V101-V110, were subsequently redesignated in the V23-V32 range, the Ju 88 V25 (NH+AK) representing the Zerstörer variant.

A Family Member – The Ju 188

As author Helmut Erfurth has already covered the history of the Ju 188 in Black Cross Vol 1: *Junkers Ju 188*, only the lead-up to the Ju 388 will be covered here.

The first actual Ju 188 prototype, the Ju 188 V1, stemmed from the Ju 88 V44 (NF+KQ)

equipped with two BMW 801G radials that were fitted to the Ju 188 which had enlarged tail surfaces. This machine, conforming to Ju 188E standard, was piloted by Flugkapitän Rupprecht Wendel on its maiden flight. It was also flown by Luftwaffe pilots, who gave the aircraft the thumbs-up.

The Ju 188 was initially thought of as only an interim solution. At that stage, it was hard to

imagine that this 'emergency solution' would prove itself to be so suitable that it would equip frontline formations until the end of the war. The aircraft performed well, was reliable, and popular with its crews. During its development, this design appeared in several variants including bomber and reconnaissance roles.

Instead of following normal alphabetical order, the Ju 188E was the first version to be

The Ju 88 V8 (D-ASCY) prototype of the Ju 88A with four-bladed airscrews.

A works model of the Ju 88B

The same model showing a total of six underwing suspensions and slatted dive-brakes.

Top left: **Following appropriate modifications, the Ju 88 V44 (NF+KQ) became the first Ju 188 prototype.**

Above: **In-flight view of the modified Ju 88 V44. The Jumo 211s were replaced by BMW 801 engines.**

Left: **The Ju 388L reconnaissance model was equipped with three cameras.**

Below: **Head-on view of the Ju 388 V1 (DW+YY) cockpit and engine nacelles. The WT 131Z *Waffentropfen* (weapon pod) was mounted beneath the fuselage.**

Bottom left: **The Ju 388 V1 was coated on upper and lateral surfaces in RLM 02 and on the undersides with RLM 65, but possibly also with RLM 76. The canopy bracings were presumably RLM 66. Call-sign letters were in black.**

Below right: **A close-up of the Ju 388 V2 with nose radar array. The weapon pod housed 2 x 20mm and 2 x 30mm cannon between which was the lower component of the periscope sight.**

delivered. The reason for this was because the Jumo 213 had not yet reached production maturity, production of this version being delayed until 1943. It was fortunate that the BMW 801 existed – it saved many a project from foundering. The following is a brief summary of the variety of sub-types of the Ju 188:

- Ju 188E: E-0 and E-1 bombers; E-2 torpedo-bomber
- Ju 188F: F-1 and F-2 long-range reconnaissance
- Ju 188G: G-0 and G-2 bombers; presumably only prototypes completed
- Ju 188H: H-2 long-range reconnaissance; project only; based on the Ju 188C
- Ju 188R: R-0 night-fighter prototype
- Ju 188A: A-0 and A-2 bombers, A-3 torpedo-bomber
- Ju 188C: C-0 with manned tail turret, alternatively remote-controlled; not built
- Ju 188D: D-1 reconnaissance, D-2 naval reconnaissance; prototypes built
- Ju 188S: S-1 high-altitude bomber with pressurised cabin, unarmed; only prototypes built. A variant was the S-1/V1 with BK 5 cannon.
- Ju 188T: T-1 reconnaissance variant based on the S-1

A total of 1,036 (confirmable) examples of this design were completed, of which 500 were of the bomber version. The three versions not listed here formed the transition to the Ju 388.

Redesignated –
The Ju 188J, K, and L Models

In September 1943, the so-called 'Hubertus Programme' was introduced. It was to provide the scope for further development of the Ju 188 into the much-improved Ju 388 – the successor that was to be built in three basic variants. As had often happened in the past, the powerplant caused some problems and consequent delays. From the autumn of 1943, the Ju 388 was one of the great hopes, besides jet aircraft, for the increasingly beleaguered Luftwaffe. In contrast to the Do 335, whose novel configuration enabled a breathtaking speed to be achieved by an aircraft with orthodox engines, the Ju 388 was expected to fulfil its role at high altitudes. The otherwise conventionally designed Ju 388, unlike the Do 335, featured a previously only very rare characteristic – a pressurised cabin that enabled a service ceiling of 13,000m (42,650ft) to be reached. High speed, coupled with the ability to operate with superiority at high altitudes, would certainly have enabled Luftwaffe losses to be reduced even in the face of increasing Allied air superiority. But overwhelming successes were not to be forthcoming.

The basis for future development that led to numerous variants of the Ju 388 were the Ju 188J, K and L, redesignated as the Ju 388. These sub-types were intended to fulfil the following roles:
- Ju 388J as day-fighter, night-fighter and day Zerstörer
- Ju 388K as high-altitude bomber, and
- Ju 388L for day-, night- and high-altitude reconnaissance

The first V-model in the Ju 388 configuration was the Ju 388LV1 – the prototype for the reconnaissance series. This aircraft originated at the end of 1943 out of parts of a Ju 188T airframe. The ensuing works trials and further testing in Rechlin made a positive impression. As a result, the ATG firm was given a contract for the conversion of ten Ju 188 airframes to Ju 388L standard, and the first of these modified aircraft was handed over to the Luftwaffe in August 1944. Initial series-production aircraft were to have been built in Merseburg, and preparations for such were almost completed at this time.

Above: **Easily recognisable as a night-fighter variant with its so-called *Hirschgeweih* (stag's antlers) radar array is this view of the Ju 388 V2.**

Right: **The Ju 388 V3 (PG+YB) prototype of the bomber variant.**

Further views of the Ju 388 V3 (PG+YB) powered by BMW 801J radials. The most noticeable difference to the Ju 388L was its extended ventral fuselage wooden bomb bay pannier. Aircraft like the Ju 388 increase the heartbeat of the aviation enthusiast. On this prototype, the markings are clearly visible on the wings and fuselage.

Chapter Seven

Ju 388 Technical Details

The original text of the *Baubeschreibung* (Construction Description) reproduced below refers to the Ju 388L-1 and J-3, and consists of the *Kurz-Baubeschreibung* (Short Construction Description) which, because of its limited extent, does not satisfactorily provide answers to all questions. Further technical details will be found in the next chapter and in the accompanying table there. The Junkers description and the *Baubeschreibung* of the Ju 388K-0 are reproduced in the original text, except that individual passages have been rearranged to provide a better overall perspective of the sub-types.

Kurz-Baubeschreibung (L-1, J-3) and *Baubeschreibung* (K-0)

General Remarks

The Ju 388 is a further development of the Ju 188 which, by reason of its high-altitude and speed capabilities, is able to operate in difficult airspace. It thereby has the advantage of proven flight characteristics, equivalent handling qualities and significantly established maintenance and well co-ordinated supplies.

For the tasks to be performed by a fast high-altitude aircraft, only a few adaptations and development measures have proved necessary for individual construction components to reduce drag and weight.

Drag Reduction

Compared to the Ju 188, the crew compartment area is smaller. The aerodynamics are improved by elimination of the B-Stand and the ventral prone position, and the adoption of a narrower cabin. Armament is reduced to the remote controlled tail H-Stand which, by its location and size is almost drag free.

High-altitude Developments

Powerplants consist of the 9-8801J-0 (BMW 801J with exhaust-gas turbo-supercharger). The crew compartment is laid out as a pressurised cabin.

Ju 388L-1

Use: Twin-engined day- or night-fighter.
Principal data: Stress Group H, Application Group 3. Permissible landing weight: 12,000kg (26,455 lb) Span: 22m (72ft 2⅛in), wing area 56m² (602.76ft²).

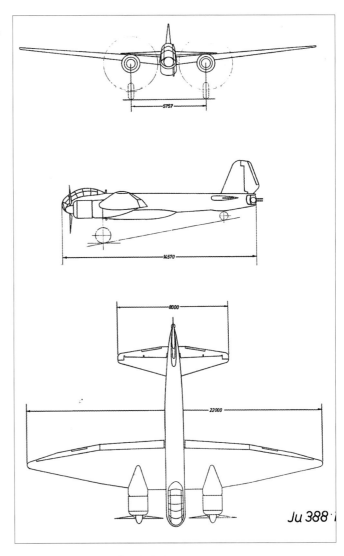

Ju 388K-1 three-view with principal dimensions. Span 22m (72ft 2⅛in), length 14.57m (47ft 9⅝in), tailspan 8m (26ft 3in), undercarriage track 5.757m (18ft 10⅜in).

Ju 388

Ju 388J-3

Use: Zerstörer and Night-fighter
Remarks: Overall construction is the same as the Ju 388L-1. Installation of another powerplant (9-8213D-1) and change in role, however, necessitated the following alterations:

Ju 388K-0

Owing to its use as a bomber, the Ju 388K has a differently oriented spectrum and differs in a number of ways from the other two series models. The *Bauanweisung* (Construction Order) was valid for a contract for 20 aircraft, and the corresponding description relative to the Ju 388K-0 had the following details:

Cockpit Area

Operating Installations (K-0): New operating installations. Levers and equipment on the operating console are similar to the Ju 188E-1.

High-altitude oxygen system: High-altitude HA-41 breathing equipment is provided for the crew of three in the crew cabin (3 x 4 spherical bottles each of 2-litre capacity) housed in the starboard wing. Installation of 16 bottles is possible (on the J and K-0).

Pressurised Cabin

Ju 388L-1 pressure-cabin: The crew compartment is laid out as a high-altitude pressurised full-vision cabin for an internal excess pressure

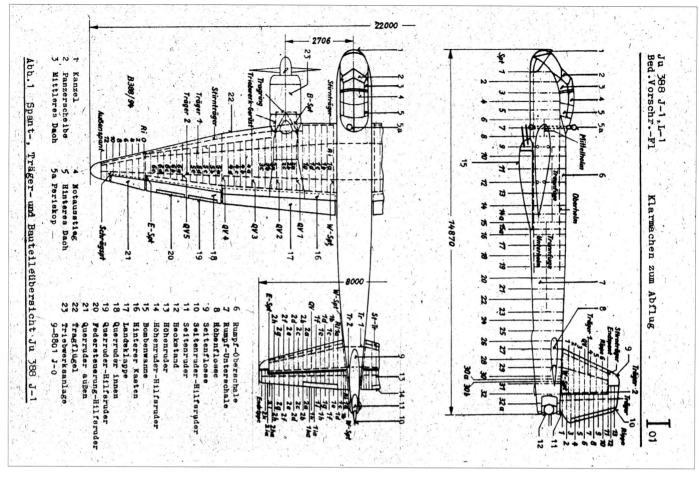

Above: **Ju 388J-1 fuselage frames and wing ribs**   Below: **Ju 388L-1 fuselage frames and wing ribs**

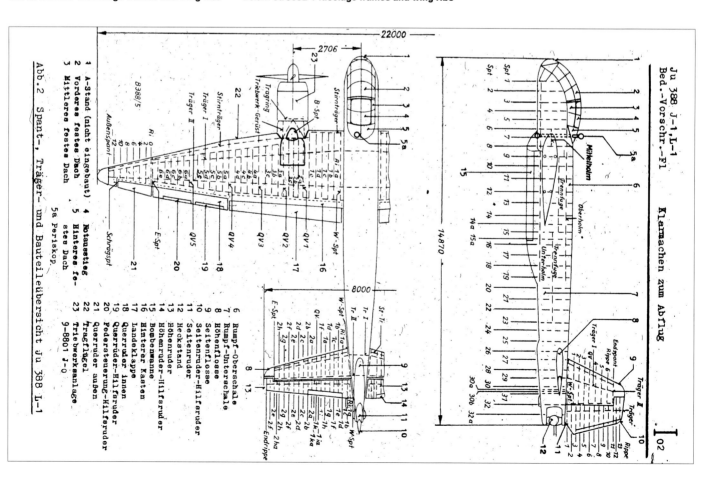

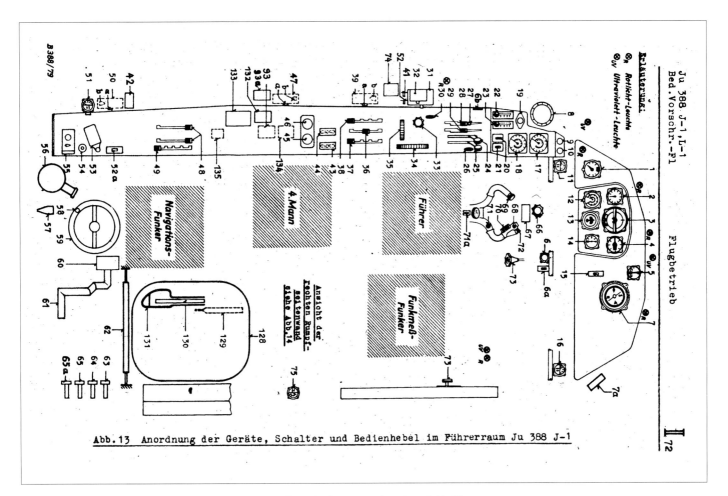

Abb.13 Anordnung der Geräte, Schalter und Bedienhebel im Führerraum Ju 388 J-1

Above: **Ju 388J-1 crew cabin and instrumentation layout**

Below: **Ju 388L-1 instrument layout on right side of cockpit**

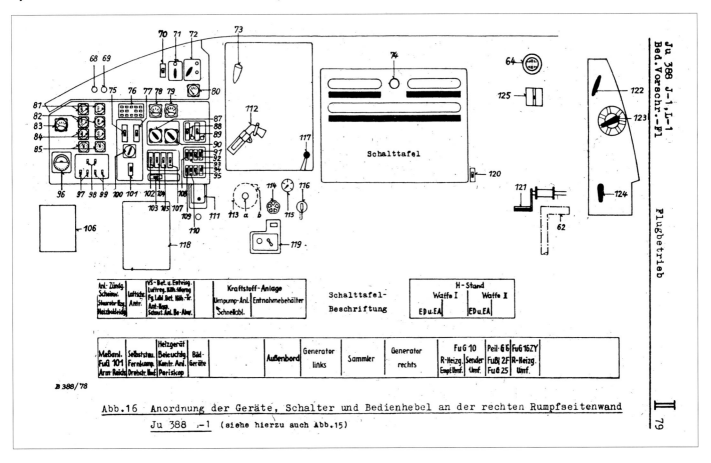

Anl. Zündg. Scheinw. Steuersch-Reg. Heizbekleidg.	Lufttech. Antr.	VS-Bet. u. Entriag. Luftreg. Küh-Wartg. Fg. Lbl Bet. Küh-Tr. Ant-Nass Schmst Anl Be-Abw.	Kraftstoff-Anlage Umpump-Anl.	Entnahmebehälter Schnellabl.	Schalttafel- Beschriftung	H-Stand				
						Waffe I EDu.EA	Waffe I EDu.EA			
Meßbel. FuG 101 Arm Reichl	Selbststeu. Fernkamp. Drehstr.Umf.	Heizgerät Beleuchtg. Kontr.Anl. Periskop	Bild- Geräte		Außenbord	Generator links	Sammler	Generator rechts	FuG 10 R-Heizg. Empf.Umf.	Peil· G 6 Sender Umf.	FuBl 2F FuG 25	FuG 16ZY R-Heizg. Umf.

Abb.16 Anordnung der Geräte, Schalter und Bedienhebel an der rechten Rumpfseitenwand

Ju 388 ↓-1 (siehe hierzu auch Abb.15)

59

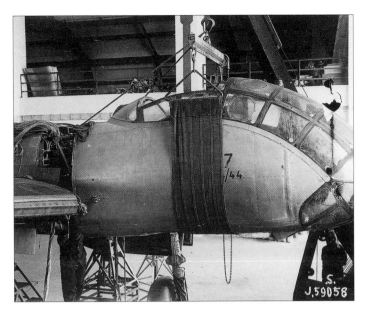

Opposite page:

Top left: **The cockpit transparencies were made up of numerous individual segments.**

Bottom left: **The instrument console in the Ju 388K-1 bomber.**

Top right: **The pilot's section of the cockpit. At top is the so-called 'oxygen shower'.**

Centre right: **A view of the lower region. In front of the pilot's stick is the console with the most important instruments. Further forward of it, the rudder pedals are visible.**

Bottom right: **Another view inside the Ju 388K cockpit.**

This page:

Above: **The cockpit segment ahead of the uncovered fuselage attachment point. Note the damage to the nose.**

Above right: **Close-up of the ventral cabin nose area – doubtless of use to the modeller.**

Lower right: **Works drawings of the Ju 388K, L and J cockpit and panelling.**

Priority 1
10a **Cockpit bolt connections**

Priority 2
1   **Front bracing**
3   **Centre bracing**
6   **Rear bracing**
8   **Emergency exit hatch**
10b **Cabin separation**
13   **Entrance hatch**
16   **Observer's seat**
17   **Radio operator's seat**
14   **Pilot's seat**

Priority 3
2   **Forward transparencies**
4   **Upper and side transparencies**
5   **Emergency vision window**
7, 9 **Other transparencies**
11   **Telescopic bombsight window**
12   **Ventral sighting window**
14   **W/T support frame**

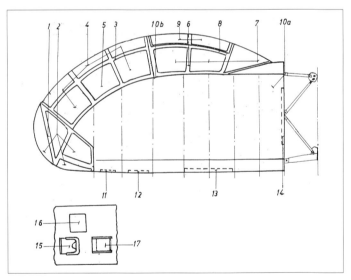

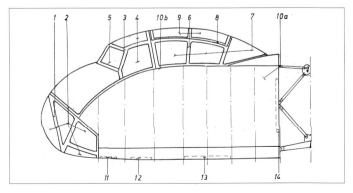

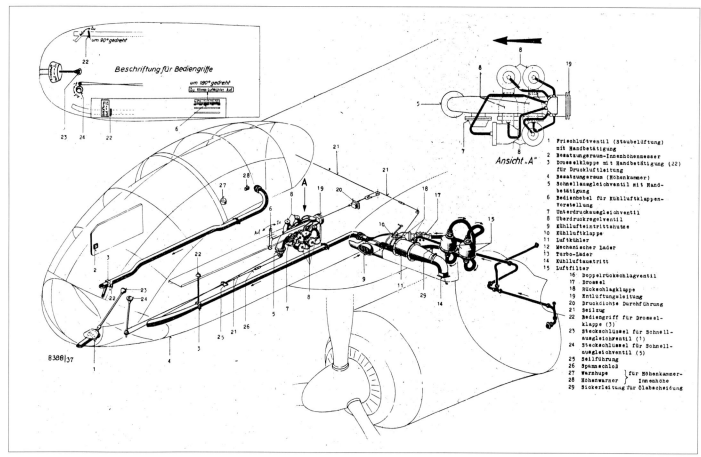

Ansicht „A"

```
1  Frischluftventil (Staubelüftung)
   mit Handbetätigung
2  Besatzungsraum-Innenhöhenmesser
3  Drosselklappe mit Handbetätigung (22)
   für Druckluftleitung
4  Besatzungsraum (Höhenkammer)
5  Schnellausgleichventil mit Hand-
   betätigung
6  Bedienhebel für Kühlluftklappen-
   Verstellung
7  Unterdruckausgleichventil
8  Überdruckregelventil
9  Kühllufteintrittshutze
10 Kühlluftklappe
11 Luftkühler
12 Mechanischer Lader
13 Turbo-Lader
14 Kühlluftaustritt
15 Luftfilter
16 Doppelrückschlagventil
17 Drossel
18 Rückschlagklappe
19 Entlüftungsleitung
20 Druckdichte Durchführung
21 Seilzug
22 Bediengriff für Drossel-
   klappe (3)
23 Steckschlüssel für Schnell-
   ausgleichventil (1)
24 Steckschlüssel für Schnell-
   ausgleichventil (5)
25 Seilführung
26 Spannschloß
27 Warnhupe    } für Höhenkammer-
28 Höhenwarner }   Innenhöhe
29 Sickerleitung für Ölabscheidung
```

Beschriftung für Bediengriffe
um 90° gedreht
um 180° gedreht
Zu Klima-Luftkühler Auf

of 0.2 atmospheres. At a flight altitude of 13km (42,650ft), internal pressure corresponds to that at 8km (26,250ft). To maintain the internal pressure, a specific quantity of engine charging air is diverted to the pressure cabin. This air, purified by a filter, also provides cabin heating. Connections for heatable clothing are also available.

The cockpit panelling consists of a double Plexiglas layer equipped with moisture-absorbing cartridges for maintaining clear vision. For astronomical navigation purposes, a few of the panels consist of Siglas panels that are also installed as duplex layers. The rear portion of the cabin hood is jettisonable. In an emergency, the entry door at the base of the cabin

can be opened by compressed air (150atm pressure) and is also jettisonable.

Crew Compartment

Ju 388K-0: This three-man crew cabin is built as a single major construction assembly and is attached to the fuselage by bolts. It has easily removable skin panels between the cabin and fuselage to enable access to the pressure-tight conduits and leads.

The three-part cockpit hood with double Plexiglas panelling is protected against moisture formation by drying cartridges. The entrance hatch is used as an emergency exit as it can be opened by compressed air and is also jettisonable.

Top left and right: **Canopy damage such as above often occurred to a greater or lesser extent.**

Above: **Schematic arrangement of the cockpit air-conditioning system (from J-1, K-1 Operating Instructions).**

Fuselage

Ju 388L-1: Of monocoque construction, the smooth sheet-metal trapezoidal fuselage has four main longerons and 36 vertical transverse frames. It is divided longitudinally into upper and lower bays. Two fuel tank compartments are located between frames 9 and 15. Additional large fuel tanks and cameras can be

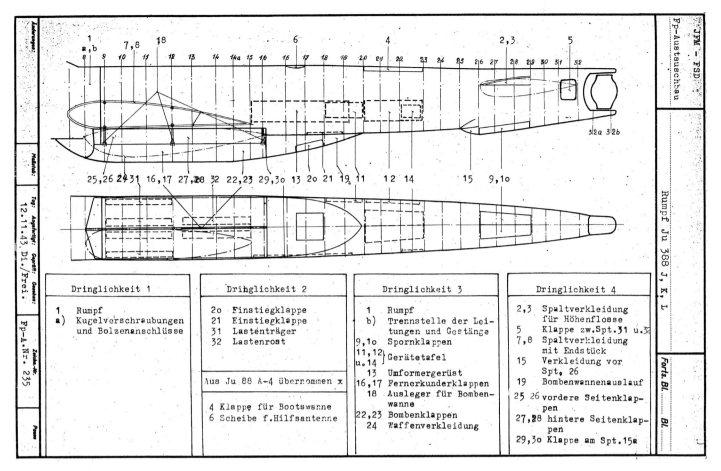

Dringlichkeit 1	Dringlichkeit 2	Dringlichkeit 3	Dringlichkeit 4
1 Rumpf a) Kugelverschraubungen und Bolzenanschlüsse	2o Einstiegklappe 21 Einstiegklappe 31 Lastenträger 32 Lastenrost Aus Ju 88 A-4 übernommen x 4 Klappe für Bootswanne 6 Scheibe f.Hilfsantenne	1 Rumpf b) Trennstelle der Leitungen und Gestänge 9,1o Spornklappen 11,12 u.14 } Gerätetafel 13 Umformergerüst 16,17 Fernerkunderklappen 18 Ausleger für Bombenwanne 22,23 Bombenklappen 24 Waffenverkleidung	2,3 Spaltverkleidung für Höhenflosse 5 Klappe zw.Spt.31 u.32 7,8 Spaltverkleidung mit Endstück 15 Verkleidung vor Spt. 26 19 Bombenwannenauslauf 25 26 vordere Seitenklappen 27,28 hintere Seitenklappen 29,3o Klappe am Spt.15a

Works drawing of the fuselage frames 8 to 32b in the Ju 388J, K and L.

The empennage region as seen on the Ju 388L (KS+TA).

Works drawing of wing trailing-edge controls and empennage surfaces.

Priority 1

1, 2	Landing flaps
3, 6, 7, 9	Ailerons
4	Trim tabs
5, 8	Spring-operated tabs
10, 11	Tailplane halves
20, 23	Elevator halves
22, 25	Trim tabs
26	Fin
29	Rudder
32	Servo-tab

Priority 4

12, 13, 16, 17	Panels
14, 18, 21, 24	End caps
28a, 30, 31	End caps
15, 19, 28	Attachment-point fillets
27, 27a	Access hatches

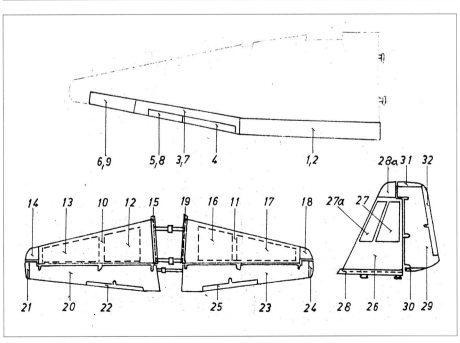

Underside port wing of the Ju 388L (RT+KI). An antenna for the FuG 217R is visible above the upper wing surface.

Rear view of the Ju 388 wing with its overwing antenna locations.

The maintenance and access hatches are visible here on this Ju 388.

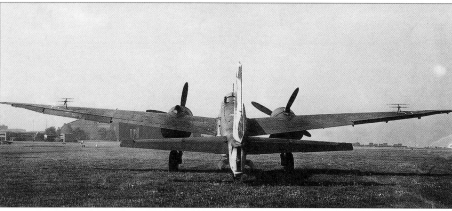

housed in the fuselage between frames 9 and 15 in a ventral trough. The remote-controlled tail armament position is at the fuselage rear behind frame 15. Entry to this area is aft of the second load-bearing bay. On the L-1 and K-0, the bomb pannier was of wood.

Ju 388J-3: Beneath the fuel tanks in the forward loading bay are the ammunition belt containers for the two MG 151 and MK 108 cannon. The weapons are located in their own weapons housing on the left side beneath the fuselage. Installed behind the second loading bay are the two 70° oblique upward-firing weapons, the tail turret being located at the rear as in the Ju 388L-1. Entry to this area is via the entrance hatch behind the second loading bay.

Empennage
Ju 388L-1: Cantilever divided tailplane assembly with internal elevator balance and coupled Flettner trim tabs adjustable from the cockpit. Centrally arranged empennage and tailplane, whose elevator and Flettner trim tabs function together in flight as an adjustable trim control surface.

The wing ailerons and flaps are of the jet-slot type. The inner portions of the landing flaps are sheet-metal covered.

Wing
Ju 388L-1: Cantilever wing. The two dihedralled halves are each attached to the fuselage by four universal joints.

Ju 388K-0: Motorwall and attachment as in the Ju 188A-2 with screw-on unitary connection feature. New partition covering and exhaust hood. Fire protection on wing upper side behind the exhaust hood.

All three – the Ju 388J, K and L – had 33 wing ribs, three spars and sheet-metal skinning.

De-icing: Kärcher unit in fuselage for elevator de-icing. Wing de-icing is by means of warm air from the powerplants. Air circulation de-icing as in Ju 188E-1. De-icing tanks are of 18 litres capacity.

Ju 388-Series Powerplants (BMW 801 – see also Ju 288)
Ju 388L-1: The 9-8801-J0 unit is installed. The BMW 801J installed here is an air-cooled 14-cylinder twin-row radial with two supercharger stages. The first stage serves as an exhaust-gas turbo-supercharger and the second serves as an engine-driven two-speed blower for ground and altitude supercharged power in the compressor air-cooling.

Engine regulation takes place automatically via the *Kommandogerät* control device with single-lever operation.
- Take-off power: 1,615hp.
- Climb and combat power: 1,472hp at sea level

and 1,430hp at 12.3km (40,355ft) rated altitude. C3 fuel is used.
- Airscrews: four-bladed VDM 912188 variable-pitch dural airscrews of 3.726m (12ft 2¾in) diameter with automatic operation.

Ju 388J-3: Installed is the 9-8213D-1 unit. The Jumo 213E installed is a water/glycol-cooled 12-cylinder hanging-Vee spark-ignition motor with two superchargers and mechanical three-speed gear-change mechanism.
- Take-off power: 1,580hp at sea level.
- Climb and combat power: 1,430hp at 10.2km (33,465ft) rated altitude.
- Airscrews: four-bladed Junkers VS 19 variable-pitch airscrews of 3.60m (11ft 9¾in) diameter with automatic operation.

Ju 388K-0: The 9-8801J-0 unit is installed. Features of the BMW 801J-1 are the same as described above.

Fuel System

Ju 388L-1 day reconnaissance aircraft: On this variant, the cameras are housed beneath the 500-litre fuel tank in the rear loading bay. In the night reconnaissance variant, a 725-litre fuel tank is to be installed in the forward loading bay and beneath it the L-attachment mechanism for eight flares. A further four flares can be mounted on two suspension points.

Fuselage tanks are capable of rapid emptying as are the right wing unprotected tanks. A 900-litre external tank on a jettisonable suspension is also possible.

Ju 388L-1 fuel tanks:
- Output tanks in left wing (415 litres) and right wing (415 litres)
- Auxiliary tanks in left wing (425 litres) and right wing (500 litres)
- Auxiliary tanks in forward fuselage (1,680 litres) and rear fuselage (500 litres).
  Total capacity: 3,935 litres.

Right: Plan views of wing and undercarriage access hatches

Below: Owing to lack of availability of the Jumo 222, the Ju 388L (RT+KD) was powered by the BMW 801TJ.

Bottom left: **BMW 801TJ engine detail.** M Baumann

Bottom right: **Engine attachment point to the aircraft.** M Baumann

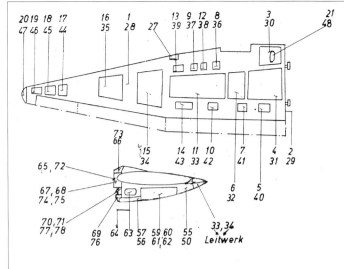

Priority 1		Priority 4	
1, 28a	Wing universal joint connections	2, 29	Attachment brackets for slot coverings
Priority 2		16 to 19	Access hatch covers
3 to 15, 34,	Access hatch covers	30 to 35	Access hatch covers
36 to 39	Access hatch covers	40 to 46	Access hatch covers
Priority 3		20, 47	End caps
1, 28b	Conduits and cables	21, 48	Boundary hatch cover
55 to 62	Undercarriage hatch covers	65, 78	Intermediate coverings

Top left and right: **BMW 801TJ details. The massive vent above the engine is the exhaust-gas outlet and beneath it the exhaust-gas turbine. Beside the latter at left is the supercharger air inlet ducting. A portion of the exhaust-gas collector ring is visible.**
Both M Baumann

Left: **Works photo of a BMW 801TJ, looking towards the rear at left.**

release, as in the Ju 188G-2. In the forward fuselage loading bay is a 725-litre tank and, in the rear bay, one of 500 litres capacity. Total capacity is 2,960 litres.

Airscrews

Ju 388K-0: Four-bladed VDM 912188 automatic variable-pitch airscrews.

Undercarriage

Ju 388L-1: The undercarriage consists of two mainwheel components and the tailwheel, each mainwheel unit retracting rearwards behind and into the lengthened engine nacelle. The 1,140 x 410mm (44.9 x 16.1in) mainwheels are fitted with individual brakes, the universally swivellable 560 x 200mm (22 x 7.9in) tailwheel being retractable as well. Undercarriage springing is provided by hydraulic-oil/compressed-air oleo legs; the tailwheel by KPZ shock absorbers.

Military Equipment
(for various Ju 388 versions)

Ju 388L-1 H-Stand: The defensive armament consists of a twin FHL 131Z in the fuselage tail. This position has an unhindered field of +/- 45°

Ju 388L-1 lubrication system: The two power-plants each have separate lubrication systems. A lubricant tank is built into each wing between frames 1 and 2 for each engine. Protected tanks each with a capacity of 136 litres or alternatively a lubricant maximum filling of 105 litres and two unprotected auxiliary tanks each of 40 litres can be installed in the left and right wing halves.

Ju 388J-3 Fuel tanks:
- Output tanks in left wing (415 litres) and right wing (415 litres)
- An unprotected outer tank in the left wing

(425 litres) and right wing (500 litres)
- An auxiliary forward fuselage tank (475 litres) and rear fuselage tank (1,050 litres). Total capacity: 3,280 litres.

Ju 388K-0: Two output tanks each of 405 litres are housed in the left and right wing halves. An auxiliary 425-litre tank without fuel quick-emptying is contained in the left wing. In the right wing is an explosion-protected 500-litre tank in an unprotected form with fuel quick-emptying facility. Until the conclusion of trials of the 500-litre explosion-protected tank, a protected tank is installed in the right wing with fuel quick-

vertical and +/- 60° horizontal traverse. Target-sighting device is the PVE 11 twin periscope housed in the crew compartment, with FA-15 power drive. It serves simultaneously as a downward observation instrument.

Cameras: Day reconnaissance aircraft cameras consisted of either 2 x Rb 20/30, 2 x Rb 50/30 or 2 x Rb 75/30. In the night reconnaissance aircraft, the cameras can be either 2 x NRb 35/25, 2 x NRb 40/25 or 2 x NRb 50/25.

Bombload: For night reconnaissance aircraft, it is possible to carry 12 illumination flares. Besides eight flares in the L-frame and four on the two wing suspension points, it is possible to carry a 900-litre drop-tank or one bomb.

Armour Protection: The pilot has a unitary seat with back and head armour-plating. The observer has back armour-plating. The radio operator has armour-plating in the rear cabin hood. The upper rear cockpit wall is armour-plated.

Armament (J-3): Fixed Zerstörer pack in flight direction beneath fuselage on the left side between frames 9 and 12, with 2 x MG 151/20 (180 rounds/gun) and 2 x MK 108 (110rpg). Oblique 70° upward-firing weapon set behind frame 15, with 2 x MG 151/20 (200rpg). Defensive tail armament is 1 x FHL 131Z in the J-2 and J-3 with +/- 45° vertical and +/- 60° horizontal traverse. Target-sighting device is the PVE 11 twin periscope and FA-15 drive operated by the radio operator.

Armament (K-0): A B-Stand with 1 x MG 151, hand loading, hand trigger, left-hand feed. With

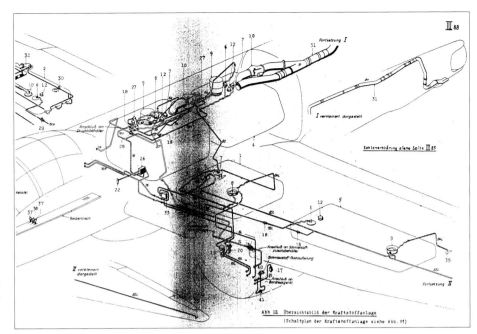

Top: **Works drawing of the Ju 388 fuel feed system.**

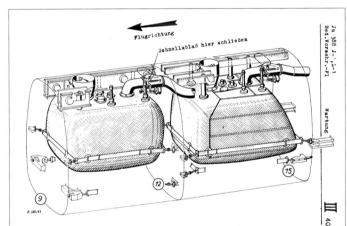

Right: **Works drawing of the two fuselage fuel tanks and quick-emptying system.**

Below: **Works drawing of the lubrication system.**

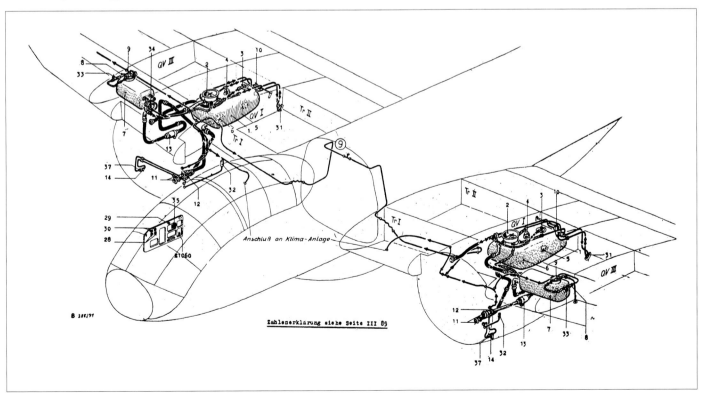

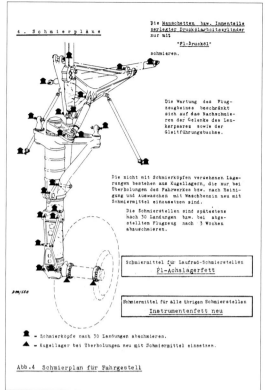

4 . Schmierpläne

Die Manschetten baw. Innenteile
zerlegter Druckölarbeitszylinder
nur mit

"Fl-Drucköl"

schmieren.

Die Wartung des Flug-
zeugbeines beschränkt
sich auf das Nachschmie-
ren der Gelenke des Len-
kerpaares sowie der
Gleitführungsbuchse.

Die nicht mit Schmierköpfen versehenen Lagerungen bestehen aus Kugellagern, die nur bei
Überholungen des Fahrwerkes bzw. nach Reini-
gung und Auswaschen mit Waschbenzin neu mit
Schmiermittel einzusetzen sind.
    Die Schmierstellen sind spätestens
nach 30 Landungen bzw. bei abgestelltem Flugzeug nach 3 Wochen
abzuschmieren.

Schmiermittel für Laufrad-Schmierstellen
Fl-Achslagerfett

Schmiermittel für alle übrigen Schmierstellen
Instrumentenfett neu

= Schmierköpfe nach 30 Landungen abschmieren.

= Kugellager bei Überholungen neu mit Schmiermittel einsetzen.

Abb.4 Schmierplan für Fahrgestell

Top left: Four-bladed VDM airscrews converted the BMW 801TJ energy into thrust. In the background is the Ju 388L (RT+KD).

Top right: **The lubrication points for the tailwheel.**

Below left: **Perspective illustration of main undercarriage leg lubrication points.**

Below: **Works drawing of the hydraulically operated undercarriage components.**

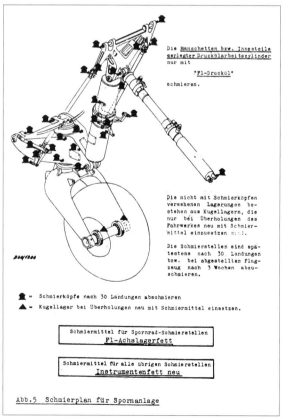

Die Manschetten bzw. Innenteile
zerlegter Druckölarbeitszylinder
nur mit

"Fl-Drucköl"

schmieren.

Die nicht mit Schmierköpfen
versehenen Lagerungen be-
stehen aus Kugellagern, die
nur bei Überholungen des
Fahrwerkes neu mit Schmiermittel einzusetzen sind.

Die Schmierstellen sind spä-
testens nach 30 Landungen
bzw. bei abgestelltem Flugzeug nach 3 Wochen abzu-
schmieren.

= Schmierköpfe nach 30 Landungen abschmieren

= Kugellager bei Überholungen neu mit Schmiermittel einsetzen.

Schmiermittel für Spornrad-Schmierstellen
Fl-Achslagerfett

Schmiermittel für alle übrigen Schmierstellen
Instrumentenfett neu

Abb.5 Schmierplan für Spornanlage

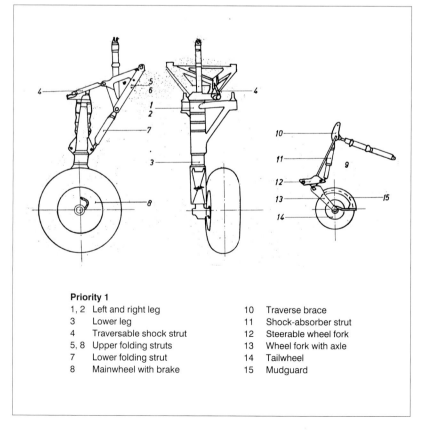

Priority 1

1, 2	Left and right leg		10	Traverse brace
3	Lower leg		11	Shock-absorber strut
4	Traversable shock strut		12	Steerable wheel fork
5, 8	Upper folding struts		13	Wheel fork with axle
7	Lower folding strut		14	Tailwheel
8	Mainwheel with brake		15	Mudguard

500 rounds belted ammunition in belt container located at right side wall in crew compartment. Front ring and bead sight. Two fixed electrically operated MG 131s (500rpg) with left and right-hand feeds in bomb bay pannier as rearward-directed defensive armament. Each has 400 rounds of belted ammunition in the left and right belt containers on fuselage side walls beneath frame 16. For target sighting, an Rf 1A or Rf 2B periscope is located ahead of the pilot in the cockpit.

Weapon Racks: Supports for the jettisonable loads are the following clasps:
- 4 x Schloss 500/XIII
- 2 x Schloss 2000/XIII B-1
- 1 x L-Gerät 8-Schloss 50 B-1
- 4 x Träger 2-Schloss 50/X B-2.

Bombload (K-0): New bomb bay door operating mechanism. Electrical priming and emergency jettison lever.

Latter in wing up to Load Condition II = M 14. Storage and cable leads for Lotfe 7H bombsight.

Armour-plating: The pilot has back and head armour. The observer has back armour. There is currently no armour planned for the radio operator. In front of the pilot is an armoured bulkhead and there are additional armoured panels in the cockpit roof.

Steering Controls

Ju 388L-1: Ailerons and elevator control takes place over the movable column with traversable arm for the control lever located at the centre of the fuselage. Rudder movement is via the rudder pedals. The trim tabs in each of these surfaces can be operated by hand-wheels. Elevator trim can also be electrically activated. Control is by means of the Patin PDS 11 two-axis control.

Ju 388K-0: This has a new type of control mechanism in the cockpit. Aileron and rudder trim tabs are activated by spring control; otherwise similar in construction to that in the Ju 188. The two-axis Patin PDS 11 provides automatic steering.

Navigation and Radio Installations

Ju 388L-1 W/T installations:
- Short- and long-wave FuG 10 with Peil G6
- FuG 25a (D/F) homing device
- FuG 101a electric altimeter
- Fu Bl 2F blind-landing equipment
- FuG 217 night-fighter warning device

Above right: **The remote-controlled FHL 131Z tail barbette.**

Right: **The pannier-mounted armament and ventral periscope of the Ju 388J-1.**

Ju 388J-3 W/T installations:
- Short- and long-wave FuG 10 wih Peil G6
- FuG 25 direction finder
- FuG 101 electric altimeter
- FuG 16Z(Y) crew intercom
- Fu Bl 2F blind-landing equipment
- FuG 220 radar sighting equipment
- SN 2 with R-installation
- FuG 350 (Naxos)
- FuG 120a (Bernhardine)
- FuG 130 (AWG)
- Safety installations as L-1 without rubber dinghy.

Ju 388K-0 W/T installations:
- FuG 10 with TZG 10 and NZG 16
- Peil G 6 with APZ A6

- FuG 25a direction finder
- FuG 101a electric altimeter
- FuG 16Z(Y) crew intercom
- Fu Bl 2F blind-landing equipment
- FuG 217 night-fighter warning device

Aircraft Electrical Systems

Ju 388L-1 electrical network: The aircraft's generator develops a power of 6,000 watts. Continuous consumption is c.2,200 watts.

The accumulators with 48 ampere-hours serve exclusively to cover power peaks.

Ju 388K-0 electrical network: Has new electrical equipment which differs in the main from the normal equipment as follows:

Detail of the Ju 388K ventral fuselage pannier and upper and lower periscope. Note the '95 Octane' stencilled beside the cockpit.

FA-15 Hydraulic Remote Control Drive (functional diagram)

Key:
A: Control apparatus
B: Power drive with oil-motor
C: Feedback (return acknowledgement) transmission
(1): Periscopic sight
(2): Directional lever for elevation movement
(3): Handwheel for lateral movement
(4): Steering/control slidegate (valve spool)
(5): Turret connecting transmission gearing
(6): Angular drive mechanism

- Heating: Heatable clothing connections in cockpit for the crew of three
- Operating: Oil and air cooling circuit. Weapons and bomb doors.
- Measurement Indicators: Fuel, lubricant, hydraulic pressure and lubricant temperatures
- Navigation and engine supervision instruments: Unitary blind-flying console III ahead of the pilot
- Pressure-maintenance and air-conditioning: Armatures and conduit layouts in wings and cockpit
- Visibility protection: Night paint in accordance with regulations for bomber aircraft
- Fuel delivery condition: Fuel feed tanks in left and right wing halves, each of 405 litres
- Auxiliary fuel tanks: 500 litres* in right wing, 425 litres in left wing, 725 litres in fuselage.
- Auxiliary tanks of 500 litres* in rear fuselage
- Lubrication system: Withdrawal tanks each of 105 litres in left and right wing
- Weapon release: 4 x Schloss 500/XII

Until the conclusion of tests of the 500-litre tank, a 425-litre tank with fuel quick-emptying is installed.

Ju 388L-1 safety installations:

- High-altitude breathing equipment: For each crew member there are four bottles in the right wing. Rubber dinghy in the fuselage pannier.
- De-icing: Wing de-icing is via warm air from the engines. Elevator de-icing via the Kärcher heater installed in the fuselage. Airscrew de-icing via the 18 litre de-icing fluid in the wing.

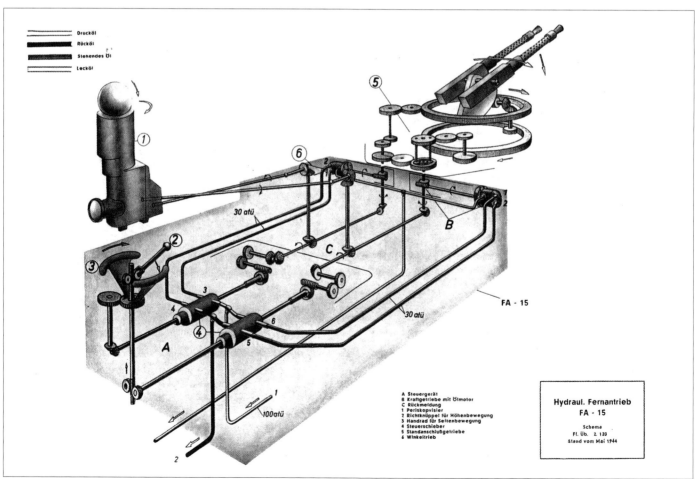

FA-15 Hydraulic Remote-Control Drive (Short Construction Description, May 1944)

The FA-15 remote control gear is a hydraulic drive for rotatable turrets with pure movement control. The pressurised oil necessary for operation is taken from the aircraft's hydraulic system.

The principal parts of the installation are:
(A) the control mechanism
(B) the force transmission
(C) the feedback (return acknowledgement)

The control mechanism A is composed of the directional transmission gearing and directional lever (2) for elevation commands, and the handwheel (3) for lateral movement commands, the slidegate (4), the worm gear, and the connection transmission for the feedback (return acknowledgement) impulses.

The slidegate is connected via pressurised-oil conduits to the rear oil-motor that drives the worm-type power unit B, which is connected by a splined shaft to the turret connection transmissions (5) and a notched-tooth connection for the return acknowledgement circuit C. The pressurised oil flows via the slidegate to the oil-motor and back over the same slidegate back into the return circuit.

The feedback serves on the one hand for adjusting the periscope sight (1), and on the other hand for the adjustment (see illustration) of the slidegate (4). Elevation movement of the control lever (2) and/or lateral movement of the handwheel (3) provide the desired commands. Depending on the vertical and lateral movement in each case, the appropriate command and acknowledging slidegate (4) responds accordingly to this movement, adjust that the slidegate valve opening so that the appropriate

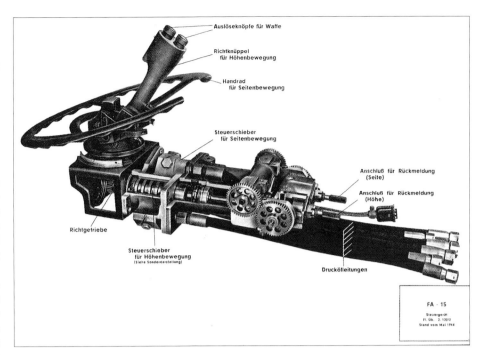

The FA-15 Steuergerät (Control Device). As of May 1944.

Auslöseknöpfe für Waffe =
   weapon activation buttons
Richtknüppel für Höhenbewegung =
   directional control column for elevation
Handrad für Seitenbewegung =
   handwheel for lateral movement control
Steuerschieber für Seitenbewegung =
   control slidegate for lateral movement
Steuerschieber für Höhenbewegung =
   control slidegate for elevation movement
Richtgetriebe =
   directional gearing
Anschluss für Rückmeldung (Seite) =
   connection for feedback circuit (lateral)
Anschluss für Rückmeldung (Höhe) =
   connection for feedback circuit (elevation)
Drucköllleitungen =
   hydraulic pressurised-oil conduits

Port wing of the Ju 388L (RT+KI) with antenna for the FuG 217R above and FuG 101 below

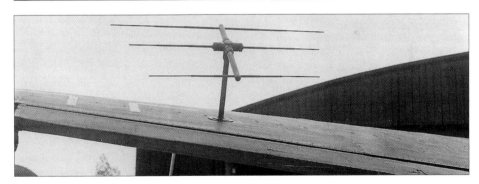

The same FuG 217R antenna seen from behind the wing trailing-edge.

Ju 388L-1 cockpit mock-up with 'Lichtenstein C-1' in the fuselage nose.

Ju 388 Technical Data Comparison

	Ju 388L-1	Ju 388J	Ju 388K-0
Powerplants			
Complete unit	9-8801J	9-8213D-1	9-8801J
Type	BMW 801TJ	Jumo 213E	BMW 801TJ
Maximum power	1,810hp at 2,700rpm	-	1,810hp at 2,700rpm
Take-off power, hp	1,615	1,750	1,615
Combat power, hp, at S/L	1,472	1,580	1,472
at rated altitude	1,430 at 12,300m (40,355ft)	1,430 at 10,200m (33,465ft)	1,430 at 12,300m (40,355ft)
Airscrews (4):	VDM 912188	Jumo VS 19	VDM 912188
Diameter	3.726m (146.7")	3.60m (141.7")	3.726m (146.7")
Dimensions			
Wingspan	22.00m (72' 4⅛")	22.00m (72' 4⅛")	22.00m (72' 4⅛")
Overall length	14.87m (48' 9½")	14.87m (48' 9½")	-
Height	4.35m (14' 3¼")	4.35m (14' 3¼")	-
Wing area, m² (ft²)	56 (602.76)	56 (602.76)	56 (602.76)
Tailspan, m (ft)	8.00 (26' 3")	8.00 (26' 3")	8.00 (26' 3")
Weights			
Equipped, kg (lb)	10,150 (22,377)	10,000 (22,046)	-
Payload, kg (lb)	5,040 (11,111)	3,960 (8,730)	-
Crew, kg (lb)	300 (661)	400 (882)	300 (661)
Take-off weight, kg (lb)	13,900 (30,644)	15,040 (33,157)	-
Wing loading, kg/m² (lbft²)	268 (54.9)	249 (51.0)	-
Max landing weight, kg (lb)	12,000 (26,455)	-	-
Performance			
Maximum speed	620km/h at 11,500m (385mph at 37,730ft)	589km/h at 11,500m (366mph at 37,730ft)	610km/h at 11,600m (379mph at 38,060ft)
Cruising speed	560km/h at 12,200m (348mph at 40,025ft)	560km/h at 12,200m (348mph at 40,025ft)	-
Range	3,100km at 11,000m (1,926 miles at 36,000ft)	2,200km at 11,000m NF (1,367 miles at 36,090ft)	1,770km (540 miles)
Service ceiling, km (ft)	12,800 (42,000)	12,850 (42,160)	12,850 (42,160)
Armament	1 x FHL 131Z (H-Stand) - -	2 x MK 108 (110rpg) 2 x MG 151/20 (180rpg) 2 x MG 151/20 (200rpg) (70° oblique upward) FHL131Z (J-2, J-3) (H-Stand)	1 x MG 131 (500 rds) (B-Stand) 2 x MG 151 (fixed, bomb pannier) -

NF = night-fighter

quantity of oil can pass through and set the oil-motor in motion. This drives the turret via the force transmissions and, in addition, over the acknowledging impulses via the angle mechanism (6), the periscope sight (1) and the acknowledging slidegate (4). It operates until such time until the acknowledging slidegate has turned so far that equal pressure again prevails on both sides of the motor block.

The weapon is always adjusted by the same amount as the directional lever or the hand-wheel is moved, so that the weapon and direction gearing always coincide. The direction command lever and handwheel can therefore be used as a rough sighting device for target capture by the periscope.

If the hydraulic oil system is switched on and the slidegate valve (4) is in the resting position, that is in the hydraulically neutral position, then with 100atm advance pressure, each side of the motor block is linked up at about 30atm, so that the feeder lines from the valve spool to the oil-motor in a position of rest are always under pressure. A quantity of oil therefore circulates and flows through the slidegate when it is in the idling condition, so that the remote-control system can be put into operation at any instant.

By adjustment of the command slidegate valve (4) a connection is made to each of the positive line and negative circuits. As a result of the ensuing pressure difference, the oil-motor is set in motion and via the feedback circuit of

the acknowledging slidegate valves (4), is again turned so far until it attains the hydraulically neutral position. The speed with which the turret turns is dependent on the twist of the command slidegate valve against that of the acknowledging slidegate valve.

In the central neutral position of the slidegate, an oil circulation exists from the plus side over the control limits to the minus side. By this means the control device has a continual flow of oil when the pressurised oil system is switched on. The return-feed and leakage oil discharge flow back into their separate feedlines.

FA-15 Control Device: The control device is configured in such a way that individual installation conditions in the airframe can be taken into account in each case. In principle, it is possible for the equipment to be either rigid or tiltable. A special characteristic of the control device, built differently for various types of weapon stands, is its differing directional angular control method and the related execution of the control column connected with it. Furthermore, the possibility exists with the B-Stand Gerät 815-Z 11 and C-Stand Gerät 815-Z 12 it is possible for electrical command transmitters for a second weapons stand to be attached.

At the control centre, the mounting option exists for directional blocking. A built-in slot or notch on the control lever guides this and hence the weapon according to the curvature guidance around the area which can be blocked. At the directional blocking point and on the directional control lever is a special mechanism which holds the control lever in the zero position and when the hydraulic oil system is switched off, appropriate hand forces at the control stick lead if necessary directly into the housing.

FA-15 Force Transmission: The force transmission is built as a worm-drive consisting of a splined shaft connection to the turret connection transmission and a connecting notched-tooth gear wheel for the feedback.

The number of revolutions of the splined shaft and that of the feedback (acknowledging) connection – at large turret tilt angles of 60°/second amounts to 300rpm. The feedback pick-up is taken directly from the worm gear. In the event that a later mechanical emergency operation is to be directed over the feedback, the pick-up for the feedback must take place at the worm gear and the necessary transmission ratio must be planned in an acknowledging transmission. This is then flanged on to the force transmission drive. The acknowledging impulses are either directly connected or are transmitted over an intermediate switching circuit at an angular gear drive.

Chapter Eight

The Ju 388 Variants

Following the brief Junkers description of the individual components of the Ju 388L/J/K, this chapter deals with the diversity of the various sub-types. In the case of the Ju 388 also, a whole range of models were planned covering a wide operational spectrum. As with other examples, however, these proposals had only been partly realised. Because of space limitations, the text deals only with the most important details.

Reconnaissance Variants

Ju 388L-1 High-altitude Long-range Reconnaissance (*Höhen-Fernaufklärer*)

- Prototype: Ju 388 V1
- The day reconnaissance variant (*Tagerkunder*) had a 1,700-litre fuel tank in the forward fuselage loading bay and a 500-litre tank in the rear bay.
- In the night-reconnaissance (*Nachtaufkärer*) role, the capacity of the forward fuel tank was reduced to 725 litres, the rear tank remaining unaltered. This variant also carried 12 flares which provided the necessary illumination when the two cameras were in operation.
- The day camera *Rüstsätze* (equipment sets) could be exchanged for night cameras. For details, (see page 67).
- Powerplants consisted of the BMW 801J (TJ), details of which are provided with the BMW 801G (see page 34).
- Defensive armament of the L-1a was a remote-controlled H-Stand equipped with the FHL 131Z – the most modern of its time. The L-1b variant additionally had a hand-operated MG 131 firing rearwards and located on the starboard side.
- The high-altitude pressurised cabin in the L-1a housed a crew of three and, in the L-1b, a crew of four.

Ju 388L-2 High-altitude Long-range Reconnaissance (*Höhen-Fernaufklärer*)

- The principal difference to the L-1 lay in its use of the Jumo 222 which would have lent a significantly improved performance to the Ju 388. The Jumo 222A/B and E/F were the intended powerplant variants.

- With the Jumo 222A/B of 46.6 litres cylinder capacity, the aircraft would have had a maximum speed of 650km/h at 7,200m (404mph at 23,620ft), a range of 2,860km at 8,000m (1,777 miles at 26,250ft), a service ceiling of 11,800m (38,710ft), an equipped weight of 11,230kg (24,758 lb) and a take-off weight of 14,850kg (32,738 lb).
- With the 2,500hp Jumo 222E/F of 49.8 litres cylinder capacity, equipped weight rose to 11,500kg (25,353 lb), take-off weight to 15,150kg (33,400 lb), maximum speed to 712km/h at 11,000m (442mph at 36,090ft) and range to 2,490km (1,547 miles). Service ceiling increased by 1,700m (5,580ft) to 13,500m (44,290ft).

Ju 388L-3 High-altitude Long-range Reconnaissance (*Höhen-Fernaufklärer*)

- The essential difference in this variant was its powerplant, the Jumo 213D-1, based on the Jumo 213E (with MW 50) intended for it. As opposed o the Jumo 222 whose power lay in the 2,000-2,500hp bracket, the Jumo 213 delivered 1,750hp that could be increased for short periods to 2,050hp with MW 50 boost. Performance level was accordingly lower, as were the weight figures.
- For the L-3, equipped weight was 10,050kg (22,156 lb), take-off weight 13,670kg (30,137 lb) and maximum speed 600km/h at 10,000m (373mph at 32,810ft). Range, however,

Baumuster Bezeichnung	Skizze	Motor und Triebwerks Bezeichnung
Ju 388 L-1 Fern-Aufklärer Nr 388/813 *)	FHL 131Z	9-8801 J-0 mit BMW 801 G
Ju 388 L-2 Fern-Aufklärer Nr 388/814 *)		9-8222 A/B mit Jumo 222 A/B /3
Ju 388 L-2 Fern-Aufklärer Nr 388/915 *)		mit Jumo 222 E/F
Ju 388 L-3 Fern-Aufklärer Nr 388/816 *)		9-8213 D mit Jumo 213 E

Ju 388L variants and their powerplants

Baumuster Bezeichnung	Skizze	Motor und Triebwerks-Bezeichnung
Ju 388 J-1 Tag-Zerstörer Nacht-Jäger Nr.388/802 x)	Ausführungsunterschiede Tag : 2 MK 103 oder 2 MG 151 Nacht: 2 MK 108 und 2 MG 151 und 2 MK 108 schräg	**9-8801 J-0** mit **BMW 801 G**
Ju 388 J-2 Tag-Zerstörer Nacht-Jäger Nr.388/804/805 x)		**9-8222A/B** mit **Jumo 222 A/B /3**
Ju 388 J-2 Tag-Zerstörer Nacht-Jäger Nr.388/806/807 x)		mit **Jumo 222 E/F**
Ju 388 J-3 Tag-Zerstörer Nacht-Jäger Nr.388/803 x)		**9-8213 D** mit **Jumo 213 E**

increased to 3,150km at 9,200m (1,957 miles at 38,185ft) so was much higher than the L-2.
- Whereas the Jumo 222 power was taken up by four-bladed VS 7 variable-pitch airscrews, the Jumo 213 drove four-bladed VS 19 airscrews.
- The L-3 variant left the final assembly lines at the rate of only 1-2 examples per month. In December 1944, the Merseburg facility delivered 37 examples of the Ju 388 reconnaissance model. A further ten Ju 388L aircraft were produced by the Weser Flugzeugbau.

Night-fighters (Nachtjäger) and Zerstörers

Ju 388J-1 Night-fighter and Zerstörer

This series of variants was intended for the day-fighter, night-fighter and heavy-fighter roles. All were powered by BMW 801TJ turbo-super-charged radials.

Ju 388J-1 Day-fighter (Tagjäger)/Zerstörer
- Prototype: Ju 388 V2
- Powerplants were the BMW 801J of 1,615hp at take-off, which could be increased for short periods to 1,810hp. Drove four-bladed VDM airscrews.

- Armament comprised 2 x MK 103 or 2 x MG 151/20 plus 2 x MG 131s in the tail barbette. The crew cabin had no armament.
- The deepened ventral fuselage bomb bay pannier was dispensed with in the reconnaissance and bomber models.
- With this variant, maximum speed was 620km/h at 11,500m (385mph at 37,730ft), range was 2,200km at 11,000m (1,367 miles at 36,090ft) and service ceiling 12,850m (42,160ft).

Ju 388J-1 Night-fighter (Nachtjäger)
- These aircraft were to have been powered by the 1,730hp BMW 801G.
- Armament comprised 2 x MK 108 (110rpg) and 2 x MG 151/20 (180rpg) firing forwards, plus 2 x MG 151/20 (200rpg) in the Schräge Musik (Jazz Music) firing 70° obliquely upward and forward.
- Radar installation consisted of the FuG 220 'Lichtenstein SN 2' with the well-known Hirschgeweih (stag's antlers) nose antenna array. This variant corresponded to the Ju 388 V2 prototype which, however, was not fitted with the oblique armament referred to. The V2/J-1 fuselage nose was similar in appearance to the Ju 88 night-fighter with SN 2 radar.
- Compared to the J-1 day fighter, equipped weight increased by 100kg (220 lb) to 10,230kg (22,553 lb), the take-off weight of 13,270kg

(29,255 lb) remaining almost identical. Because of the nose antenna array, maximum speed dropped to 589km/h (366mph), range was 2,160km at 11,000m (1,342 miles at 36,090ft), the service ceiling of 12,550m (41,175ft) being slightly less than that of the day-fighter.

Ju 388J-2 Day-fighter (Tagjäger)/Zerstörer
Technical difficulties with the remote-controlled tail barbette led to it not being installed in the J-1 variant initially. The exception, however, was the Ju 388 V2, and once the problems had been solved, the H-Stand was scheduled for installation in the J-2 series.

- Whereas the J-1 variant was powered by the BMW 801, the J-2 was to have had the 2,000hp Jumo 222A/B.
- Armament of the J-2 day fighter was to have comprised 2 x MK 103 or 2 x MG 151/20 in a pannier beneath the fuselage, together with 2 x MG 131 in the tail barbette.
- For this variant, equipped weight was 10,120kg (22,311 lb), take-off weight 14,177kg (31,255 lb), maximum speed 650km/h (404mph), range 2,000km at 8,000m (1,243 miles at 26,250ft) and service ceiling 11,900m (39,040ft).
- Dimensions were the same as the J-1 variant.

Ju 388J-2 Night-fighter (Nachtjäger)
The completely altered operational spectrum required technical equipment appropriate to this task. The J-2 therefore featured the FuG 220 'Lichtenstein SN 2' night-fighter radar with the Hirschgeweih (stag's antlers) antenna array, which reduced maximum speed to 626km/h at 7,200m (389mph at 23,620ft) with its Jumo 222 powerplants.

- Armament of the night-fighter, with its 2 x MK 108 and 2 x MG 151/20 in the ventral fuselage tray, differed from the Zerstörer/day-fighter through its 2 x MK 108 oblique upward-firing cannon.
- In contrast to the reduction in performance, weights increased due to the additional armament and electronic equipment installations. Equipped weight rose by 1,115kg (2,458 lb) to 11,235kg (24,769 lb) and take-off weight to 14,362kg (31,662 lb). Range was reduced by 250km (155 miles) to 1,850km (1,150 miles), the 11,600m (38,060ft) service ceiling being somewhat less than that of the day-fighter.

The actual number of the J-2 variants built is unfortunately not definitely known. In the event that these actually left the final assembly lines, the total could only have amounted to single examples due to the shortage of Jumo 222 powerplants.

Ju 388J-2 Zerstörer/Day-fighter (*Tagjäger*)

This variant, powered by the 49.8 litre capacity 2,500hp Jumo 222E/F, was suitable for high-altitude operations and had increased weight and performance figures over that of the Jumo 222A/B-powered sub-type mentioned above.

- Armament corresponded to that of the Jumo 222A/B-powered J-2 Zerstörer/day-fighter.
- Equipped weight of this variant was 280kg (617 lb) more, at 11,400kg (25,132 lb) and take-off weight 323kg (712 lb) more, at 14,500kg (31,967 lb).
- Maximum speed was 710km/h at 11,500m (441mph at 37,730ft), but range was 320km (199 miles) less, at 1,680km (1,044 miles), the service ceiling of 13,600m (44,620ft) being rather higher.

Ju 388J-2 Night-fighter (*Nachtjäger*)

- Powerplant of this variant was likewise the Jumo 222E/F.
- The armament of 2 x MK108 and 2 x MG151/20 in the fuselage gondola plus 2 x MK108 oblique upward-firing cannon and the remote-controlled tail barbette was the equivalent of the previous J-2 night-fighter standard.
- Equipped weight was 11,565kg (25,496 lb), take-off weight 14,690kg (32,386 lb); range at cruising speed, 2,570km (1,597 miles) and service ceiling 13,250m (43,800ft).
- Like its predecessor, radar equipment was the FuG 220 'Lichtenstein SN 2'.

It is also doubtful whether any examples of this variant were actually built. If so, they would probably have been limited to single examples since the Jumo 222E/F represented an even later development stage than the already scarce Jumo 222A/B. It should be noted that the armament details are often contradictory, not only in published literature but also in original documents. In this respect, for whatever the reason, decisions must have been taken that were later countermanded when new priorities were decided upon.

Ju 388J-3 Zerstörer/Day-fighter (*Tagjäger*)

The most important difference between this and previous variants was the use of the Jumo 213. According to the Junkers Short Construction Description, the entire 9-8213D-1 engine unit had the Jumo 213E with MW 50 injection. Take-off power was 1,750hp, with climb and combat power of 1,580hp near the ground and 1,430hp at 10,200m (33,465ft). The engine drove four-bladed Junkers VS 19 airscrews of 3.6m (11ft 9¾in) diameter.

- Fuel was housed in six tanks with a total capacity of 3,280 litres.
- Forward-firing armament, designated as the *'Starrer Zerstörersatz'* (fixed destroyer set) located on the port side beneath the fuselage

between frames 9 and 15, consisted of 2 x MK108 and 2 x MG151/20. Other sources mention the use of 2 x MK103 cannon. In addition to these weapons, the J-3 also had an FHL 131Z tail barbette.
- In terms of performance, a maximum speed of 617km/h at 10,200m (383mph at 33,465ft) was possible. Range was 2,330km at 9,200m (1,386 miles at 30,185ft) and a service ceiling of 12,500m (41,010ft) was quoted.

Ju 388J-3 Night-fighter (*Nachtjäger*)

- The Jumo 213 mentioned above was also the powerplant of this variant.
- According to the Junkers Short Construction Description, armament was 2 x MG151/20 and 2 x MK108. In this document the so-called upward oblique armament housed behind fuselage frame15 consisted of 2 x MG151/20, whereas other documents list 2 x MK108 instead.
- In contrast to the J-1 and J-2 night-fighters, the J-3 was equipped with the FuG 228 'Lichtenstein SN 3' radar and *'Morgenstern'* (morning star) antenna dipoles, fundamentally altering the appearance of the fuselage nose into a sharp point which increased the fuselage length to 16.29m (53ft 5⅜in). Together with the antenna of the tail warning device, fuselage overall length was increased to 17.7m (58ft 0⅞in).
- Performance data for this night-fighter included a maximum speed of 585km/h at 10,200m (363mph at 33,465ft), a range of 2,400km (1,491 miles) and a service ceiling of 12,000m (39,370ft). As a means of increasing engine power, a 150-litre MW 50 tank was scheduled for installation in each wing half, and to provide greater range, 2 x 700-litre drop-tanks were proposed.

Ju 388J-4 Zerstörer/Heavy Night-fighter (*Schwerer Nachtjäger*)

Of no less interest was this proposed variant which would have been a really heavy piece of ordnance had it not remained on the drawing board. Conceived as a night-fighter, it was to have been armed with two 5cm *Bordkanone* consisting of either 2 x MK214 or BK5 cannon housed in a weapon pod offset beneath the fuselage. Experience with it had already been gained in the Ju 88P-4 (1 x BK5). Installation weight of the weapons together with all the equipment necessary for operation would have been 1,200kg (2,646 lb) without the ammunition. The Rheinmetall BK5, developed from the KWK 39 *Kampfwagen-kanone* (armoured car or tank cannon) as a competitor to the Mauser MK214, was one of the close contenders for selection. This weapon was also envisaged for the Ju 288.

Various components of the MK214, among them the breech barrel, also stemmed from the KWK 39. With both weapons, the Ju 388 could have been used in combat against ground as well as air targets. Whether attacks against

enemy bombers would actually have been as successful as expected is a matter of conjecture. In view of the increasing numbers of escort fighters, the operational use of such lumbering 'war elephants' despite coverage by single-engined fighters would also have meant significant losses for the Ju 388.

One example illustrating the success of this large-calibre aircraft armament occurred during the period between February and April 1944, when the Me 410A-2/U4 (armed with 1 x BK 5) was successful in downing 29 Boeing B-17s and 4 Martin B-24s for 9 of its own losses.

There were undoubtedly individual successes, but this was not the general rule. The mass use of the R4M air-to-air rocket projectile would have been far more effective. Heavy-calibre weapons also suffered from technical problems. The MK214A – the letter A signifying aircraft armament – had the serious disadvantage whereby the weapon had to be loaded by hand on the ground prior to take-off. Consequently any eventual blockage in flight could not be cleared – a circumstance that the J-4 designers only reluctantly accepted.

In relation to the powerplant, alternative weapons or other equipment, no information is currently available.

Bomber Variants

Ju 388K Bomber

The Ju 388K was conceived for a very different field of operation. This bomber variant began its trials with the Ju 388 V3. Its dimensions corresponded to the Ju 388L, but its equipment differed considerably from that sub-type.

- The underslung bomb pannier made of wood had the following bomb clasps: 2 x Schloss 500/XII, 2 x Schloss 2000/XIII B-1, an L-Gerät 8-Schloss 50 B-1 and 4 x Schloss 50/X B-2 installations. Added to this was a new bomb door operating mechanism, the electrical blind-sharp setting adjustment, as well as the emergency jettison lever and the Lotfe 7H bombsight.
- Defensive armament in the cockpit roof consisted of a movable MG 131 (500 rds) in the B-Stand. Two further MG 131s as fixed rearward-firing weapons operated by remote-control were located in the bomb pannier.
- Powerplants of the Ju 388K-0 and K-1 were 9-8801J-0 units consisting of the BMW 801G driving four-bladed VDM airscrews.
- The fuel was contained in six fuselage tanks of various sizes with a total capacity of 2,960 litres. Up to the end of trials with the explosion-protected 500-litre tank, 425-litre tanks with fuel quick-emptying were installed as an interim solution. Fuel quantity would have been reduced in this case to 2,885 litres.

Ju 388K-1 Bomber

This series variant differed in the following ways:

- Planned powerplants were the BMW 801J (TJ) and BMW 801TM with a new turbo-supercharger with which power would have been brought closer to the 2,000hp mark. The engine project, however, was cancelled in 1944.
- In appearance, the Ju 388K-1 and L-1 were largely identical. Both were fitted with the deepened wooden fuselage bomb bay pannier capable of carrying a 3,000kg (6,614 lb) bombload.
- Armament corresponded to that of the Ju 388K-0. The K-1 was additionally equipped with the FHL131Z tail barbette.
- Equipped weight was 10,250kg (22,597 lb), take-off weight 14,275kg (38,471 lb), maximum speed 610km/h at 11,600m (379mph at 38,060ft), maximum range at cruising speed, 1,770km (1,100 miles) and service ceiling 12,850m (42,160ft).

Ju 388K-2 Bomber

This variant, based on the use of the 2,000hp Jumo 222A/B or alternatively the Jumo 222E/F, did not get beyond the project stage.

- With the Jumo 222A/B as powerplant, equipped weight was 11,215kg (24,725 lb), take-off weight 16,000kg (35,274 lb), maximum speed 635km/h at 12,000m (395mph at 39,370ft), range at cruising speed 2,080km (1,292 miles) and service ceiling 11,700m (38,385ft).
- With the 2,500hp Jumo 222E/F, corresponding calculations gave an equipped weight of 11,545kg (25,452 lb), take-off weight 15,930kg (35,119 lb), maximum speed 695km/h at 11,500m (432mph at 37,730ft), range at cruising speed 1,800km (1,118 miles) and service ceiling 13,500m (44,290ft).

Possibly only one example in this configuration was completed, but its existence cannot be definitely confirmed.

Ju 388K-3 Bomber

The principal difference between this sub-type and foregoing variants was the switch to the Jumo 213 engine. In all probability, the complete power unit was the 9-8213D-1 bomber engine.

- Dimensions corresponded to those of the K-series described above.
- In this variant, equipped weight was 10,080kg (22,222 lb), take-off weight 14,400kg (31,746 lb), maximum speed 590km/h at 10,900m (367mph at 35,760ft), range 2,160km at 9,200m (1,342 miles at 30,185ft) and service ceiling 12,450m (40,850ft). All data were estimates as the project was never completed.

Ju 388M Torpedo-Bomber

To conclude the Ju 388 series, mention must be made of the Ju 388M torpedo-bomber. Based on the Ju 388K version, the Ju 388M-1 did not incorporate the deepened bomb pannier, being equipped only with an ETC 2000 fitting for carriage of the Blohm & Voss L10 *Friedensengel* (Peace Angel) winged glide-torpedo. A few pre-production examples of this aircraft were reportedly under construction at the end of the war, but no definitive information on this is available.

This completes the overall picture of the planned Ju 388 versions and variants. Only a very few of the variants described were actually built. In terms of details, the documents are often incomplete and the sources partly contradictory. It would be well worth while to provide a fully comprehensive history of this aircraft, but the unsatisfactory documentation makes this extremely difficult to achieve. Anyone who is able to clarify any of the unresolved points is requested to notify the author via the publisher.

Baumuster Bezeichnung	Skizze	Motor und Triebwerks- Bezeichnung
Ju 388 K-1 Nr. 388/809 x)		9-8801J-0 mit BMW 801 G
Ju 388 K-2 Nr. 388/810 x)		9-8222A B mit Jumo 222A/B
Ju 388 K-2 Nr. 388/811 x)		mit Jumo 222E/F
Ju 388 K-3 Nr 388/812 x)		9-8213 D mit Jumo 213 E

Left: **The Ju 388K variants and their powerplants.**

Opposite page:

The Ju 388 final assembly/manufacturing plan in the Junkers illustration of 27th September 1944.

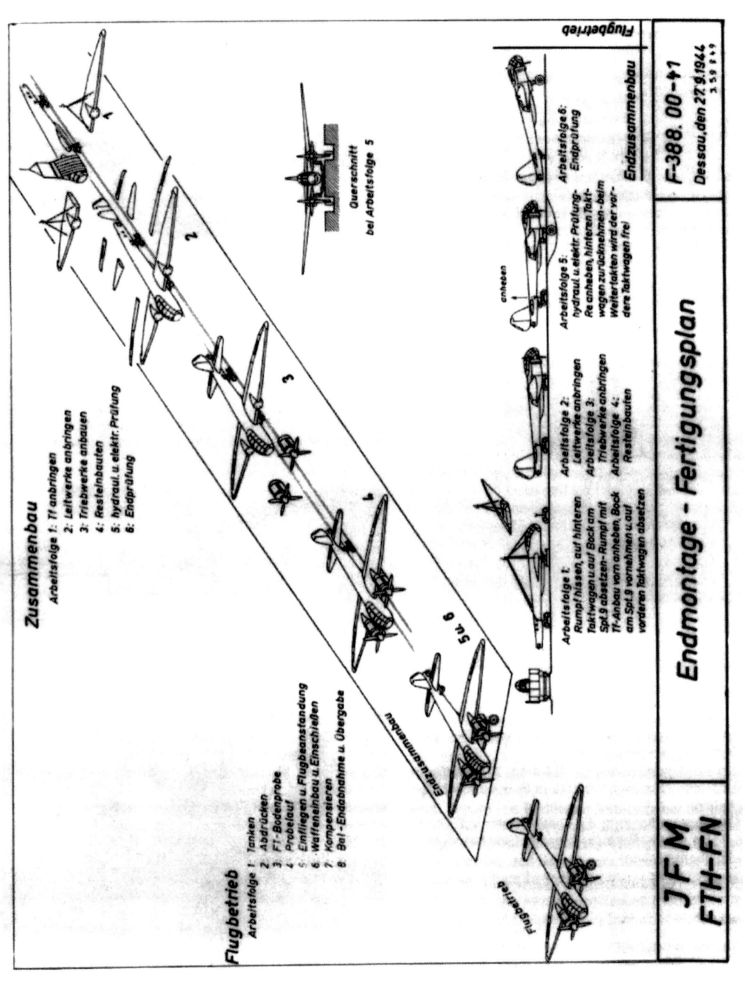

Zusammenbau

Arbeitsfolge 1: Tf anbringen
2: Leitwerke anbringen
3: Triebwerke anbauen
4: Resteinbauten
5: hydraul. u. elektr. Prüfung
6: Endprüfung

Flugbetrieb

Arbeitsfolge 1: Tanken
2: Abdrücken
3: FT-Bodenprobe
4: Probelauf
5: Einfliegen u. Flugbeanstandung
6: Waffeneinbau u. Einschließen
7: Kompensieren
8: Bel.-Endabnahme u. Übergabe

Querschnitt
bei Arbeitsfolge 5

Flugbetrieb

Endzusammenbau

Arbeitsfolge 1:
Rumpf hissen, auf hinteren
Taktwagen u. auf Bock am
Spt.9 absetzen – Rumpf mit
Tf-Anbau vorn anheben, Bock
am Spt.9 vornehmen u. auf
vorderen Taktwagen absetzen

Arbeitsfolge 2:
Leitwerke anbringen

Arbeitsfolge 3:
Triebwerke anbringen

Arbeitsfolge 4:
Resteinbauten

Arbeitsfolge 5:
hydraul. u. elektr. Prüfung-
Re anheben, hinteren Taktwagen zurücknehmen – beim
Weitertakten wird der vor-
dere Taktwagen frei

Arbeitsfolge 6:
Endprüfung

F-388.00-41
Dessau, den 27.9.1944

Endmontage - Fertigungsplan

JFM
FTH-FN

Chapter Nine

The Ju 388 in Series Production

Production plans, as with the Ju 288, were drawn up with enthusiasm, but in the case of the Ju 388 differed considerably from what had originally been proposed. Three basic versions were to have left the production centres. The basis for these was the so-called 'Hubertus Programme' which envisaged building as quickly as possible a high-altitude version of the Ju 188 in the form of the Ju 388.

Ju 388L Production

The first machine to leave the final assembly line was the Ju 388 V1. Initially, the ATG plant at Merseburg completed ten Ju 388L-0 pre-production aircraft, which stemmed from Ju 188S airframes. These were followed by a contract for several hundred examples of the L-1, divided into the Ju 388L-1a with a three-crew pressurised cabin and the L-1b with a four-crew pressurised cabin. Powerplant of the L-1 was the BMW 801, for the L-2 the Jumo 222, and for the L-3 the Jumo 213.

Up to the end of 1944, Merseburg had manufactured 37 Ju 388L aircraft including one or two examples of the L-3. A further ten Ju 388Ls left the Weser Flugzeugbau assembly lines – five each in November and December 1944.

According to a list compiled in September 1944 documenting aircraft that entered the Luftwaffe inventory, there were a total of 3,821 various types. Of these, there were just three Ju 388 pre-production machines. From Arado, 18 examples of the Ar 234 went to the Luftwaffe. By contrast, manufacture of the Do 24, Ju 87, He 111, Hs 129, Ju 352 and Me 410 was ended that month.

Ju 388J Production

The first prototype of this Zerstörer/night-fighter version was the Ju 388 V2. This stage of the air war called for aircraft with good performance at high altitudes, the Ju 388 having been especially selected for this purpose in order to combat the much-feared Boeing B-29 bomber. A giant at that time, it came to be used with devastating results against Germany's ally Japan, and was expected to appear over the skies of Germany at the turn of 1944/45 – a worrying prediction that did not become a reality.

The Ju 388 V2, which began flight-testing in January 1944, was followed by the V4 and V5 prototypes – the 2nd and 3rd of this series. Only the Ju 388J-1 variant went into production in

1944 but was abandoned a short while later as a result of the new armaments guidelines in November of that year. Other sources report that series production was to start in January 1945 and that corresponding preparations were stopped in December 1944. It can therefore be assumed that, at most, only a handful of the Ju 388L version left the final assembly lines. However, because of incomplete documentation, this cannot be verified.

Ju 388K Production

This bomber version first appeared in the shape of the Ju 388 V3 prototype that made its maiden flight in January 1944. In July of the same year, ten pre-production examples as well as 5 Ju 388K-1s left the assembly lines. On the other hand, the K-2 and K-3 variants did not become a reality. The stop placed on production at the beginning of 1945 also applied to the Ju 388K. To complete the picture, an undetermined but insignificant number of Ju 388M torpedo-bombers of a pre-production batch were in the process of manufacture when the stop order was made. Total Ju 388 production was therefore as follows:

- The five (V1 to V5) prototypes, of which three were of the Ju 388J version
- Ju 388L: 37 aircraft delivered from Merseburg from October 1944, plus ten by Weser in Bremen from November 1944.
- Ju 388J: Only the V2, V4 and V5 definitely confirmable
- Ju 388K: ten of the K-0, 5 K-1 and presumably only one K-2 prototype
- Ju 388M: A few machines under construction but not completed.

A maximum of 70 to 75 Ju 388s of all versions were built – an extremely small number compared with the originally planned production quantities. According to the *Jägerstab* (Fighter Staff) plans of 8th July 1944, 300-400 Ju 388s were to have left the production centres. Comparative figures for the Ju 88 were 180 per month, and 50 per month for the He 219. As mentioned above, only three Ju 388Js have been definitely confirmed as being completed, the majority of the few Ju 388s produced having consisted of the Ju 388L reconnaissance version.

It is also interesting to consider the negotiations that took place between Germany and

Japan concerning the licence manufacturing rights for the Ju 388. The Japanese list was long and the Ju 388 formed only one of the many items. Licence requests for other Junkers products were also submitted, among them for the Ju 288 and Ju 390 aircraft, the Jumo 222, Jumo 223 and the then highly modern 109-004 turbojets. Manufacturing plans and various construction samples were to have been taken to Japan by submarine – proposals that in the course of a rapidly deteriorating war situation were very rarely accomplished. Only a few submarines were able to make the long sea voyage to far-off Nippon and the plans for large-scale production on Japanese territory remained as such – just plans.

ment.

Chapter Ten

The Ju 388 in Service Trials

Erprobungskommando 388

As already related, the Ju 288 programme had been officially terminated in mid-1943. This left a gap which needed to be filled as soon as possible. The Ju 188 was initially considered, which itself, as far as planning went, was to have been succeeded by the Ju 388, the latter consisting principally of a high-altitude derivative of the Ju 188. In order to evaluate the three basic Ju 388 versions for their operational suitability, EK 388 was formed with effect from 15th July 1944. Towards the end of the month, the advance detachment took over the installations intended for this purpose in the E-Stelle Rechlin where three of the eight Ju 388s on hand were earmarked for the Test Detachment. Soon afterwards, the EK received new guidelines concerning the extent of the trials to be undertaken. In October 1944 came the directive to concentrate solely on the night-fighter variant.

In an official document dated 29th July 1944, the following aircraft are listed: 230 153, 230 155, 300 004*, 300 005*, 300 008*, 300 009*, and 300 291 (those marked with an asterisk are Ju 388L aircraft).

A Junkers report of 1st August 1944 lists the following aircraft with their respective flying hours accomplished to date:

230 153	K-0	(KS+TC)	25 hours
230 155	K-0	(KS+TE)	8 hours
300 002	L-0		27 hours
300 004	L-0		30 hours
300 005	L-0		55 hours
300 007	L-0		48 hours
300 009	L-0		28 hours
300 291			15 hours

The two reports contain differences. In the Junkers report, 300 002 and 007 are listed, whereas 008 is missing.

Hardly had EK 388 established itself in Rechlin than the E-Stelle became the target for attack by the 8th USAAF. The raid took place on 25th August 1944 and, in accordance with US strategy, was conducted during daylight hours. Besides Rechlin, Mission 570's targets were the oil industry and technical installations in Pölitz on which Boeing B-17 bombers of the 3rd Bomb Division were engaged. Of the 380 bombers that took off, for various reasons only 354 appeared over the target. Shortly after noon, the air-raid sirens sounded in Rechlin, over which 179 B-17s appeared and dropped

396 tons of bombs. Approaching from the direction of Stettin, the bombers of the 486th and 487th BG opened their bomb doors. This was the initial phase of a 20-minute attack that cost the lives of 20 individuals. The material damage was extensive and all hangars were hit. Flying operations were transferred to the outstation airfields at Lärz and Roggenthin while repairs were carried out. But the attackers also suffered losses. The bomber streams, escorted by 215 Mustangs and Thunderbolts, lost eight B-17s and another had to be written off after its return to England. No less than 182 B-17s suffered some damage, 64 of the crews went missing, and ten returned wounded to their bases, adding to the loss of four P-47 escort fighters. The comparatively small enemy losses were attributed to the increasing weaknesses of the *Reichsverteidigung* defences. Throughout the entire raid, the formation attacking Rechlin remained immune from fighter opposition, only the defensive flak having any effect.

A Junkers report of 31st August 1944 lists three of the above Ju 388s as either destroyed or damaged as the result of attack, namely:

230 155 – 70% damaged due to flying debris
300 007 – destroyed by fire
300 291 – also destroyed by fire.

It also mentions that 300 005 sustained engine damage in Stolp on 30th August 1944 due to a belly-landing.

According to the Junkers report of 2nd October 1944, at the end of September EK 388 possessed the following aircraft:

230 153 K-0   300 009 L-0   340 081 L-1   340 084 L-1
340 085 L-1   340 086 L-1   500 005 L-1/V5

As a result of the attacks, EK 388 recorded two Ju 388s as total losses and one severely damaged, in addition to the seven on hand. Testing activities were affected by American air raids, weather-related delays and the poor condition of aircraft delivered to them.

During service trials, the optimistic expectations of the Ju 388 were exposed. Their BMW 801 radials failed to bring much increase in performance. As a consequence, on 14th February 1945, the order was issued for disbandment of EK 388, which had existed for only half a year. Personnel were reassigned to KG 76 or to EK 335. On the same day, EK 335 was even

scheduled to be dissolved, but this order was rescinded shortly afterwards, as the Do 335 was also to function as a stopgap in the Führer Emergency Programme in the event that the hopes placed in the Me 262 could not be fulfilled. For EK 388, however, this meant an irrevocable disbandment.

Evaluation of monthly reports referring to EK 388, the following Ju 388 aircraft associated with this organisation can be confirmed:

Ju 388 W-Nr	Total flying hrs mins		Status 1944 as of Month	Remarks
230 153	22	45	September	
300 009	90	44	October	
300 292	-	-	-	No information
340 081	26	06	October	
340 083	-	-	September	Somersaulted in Fürth on 11.9.1944, 65% damaged
340 084	43	29	October	
340 085	43	55	November	
340 086	6	03	November	
340 087	26	47	October	
340 088	28	27	November	
340 089	-	-	October	Only 5hrs 35mins recorded that month
340 090	11	55	October	
340 093	5	50	November	
340 094	12	20	November	
500 001	2	03	October	
500 005	45	52	September	

The Versuchsverband der ObdL

This Experimental Formation of the Oberbefehlshaber der Luftwaffe (Luftwaffe C-in-C) was established in March 1942 and was renamed the *Versuchsverband OKL* (for Oberkommando der Luftwaffe = Luftwaffe Supreme Command) in 1944, until its disbandment in April 1945. It tested a whole series of aircraft types, among them the Ar 234, Ar 240, Bv 141, Do 335, Fh 104, He 111, Ju 86, Ju 88, Ju 188, Ju 290, Me 109, Me 110, Me 262 and Me 410 as well as various enemy aircraft. The Ju 388 expanded the Junkers list, and in this connection it is known that of three examples of the Ju 388L, one carried the identification T9+DL. Integration of the Ju 388 into the *Verband* took place at the end of 1944, consisting exclusively of the Ju 388L. Nothing has been unearthed to date concerning trials with the Ju 388J and K, except for the fact that no Ju 388s were flown by regular frontline units.

Chapter Eleven

Allied Booty

Testing the Captured Ju 388s

During the Allies' advance across territory still in the hands of German troops, as well as within the borders of Germany itself, they encountered various extremely important items of weapons technology. Specialist teams that had been tasked to seek out such information had followed closely behind the combat forces in order to secure highly developed technology or related documentation. This system proved highly effective and was successfully employed by the Americans, British, French and Russians. It often led to a veritable contest to secure important knowledge and information for one's own country. Such personnel as a rule, unlike frontline troops, were competent to recognise the technical value of a particular make of tank, aircraft or whatever. Documentary evidence exists to show that, all too often, extremely important discoveries fell victim to one's own soldiers who either acted as souvenir hunters and wilfully destroyed an aircraft important for future investigation, or else misused it for shooting practice out of sheer boredom. So for engineers and scientists, many opportunities to examine the enemy's technology were thwarted. A further field of activity was the search for scientists and technicians who had been engaged in the field of aeronautics. Jet aircraft and rocket technology were the main priorities, and with regard to the former, 'Watson's Wizards' gained legendary fame. The list of aircraft that were to be transported for testing in Allied countries grew steadily, the

Americans using the escort aircraft carrier *Reaper* to transport selected aircraft across the Atlantic.

Before these highly modern spoils could give up their secrets, large distances had first to be covered. The French seaport of Cherbourg became the collection point for aircraft selected for shipping to the USA. For the onward journey, the *Reaper* stood ready. In rapid succession, the cream of German aircraft manufacture was assembled on its deck, consisting of 40 aircraft of the most diverse types. On the deck of the escort carrier were four Ar 234Bs, ten Me 262s, one Ju 88G, one Ju 388, three He 219s, four Fw 190Ds, five Fw 190Fs, one Ta 152H, three Me 109s, one Doblhoff WNF 342 and two Fl 282 helicopters, one Me 108 and the two Do 335s (numbered 8 and 35 on the *Reaper*). Added to these was a reconnaissance Mustang that had been modified by the 9th USAAF and was to serve as a prototype in America. A whole series of aircraft were loaded on board merchant ships to the USA, among them several Me 163s and the He 162 *Volksjäger* (People's Fighter). The legendary Ju 290 *Alles Kaputt* (Everything Destroyed) was even flown over. In addition to all the German spoils, there were other aircraft types of Italian origin and, in much greater numbers, equipment captured from the Pacific theatre. Of course, it wasn't enough to lash the aircraft to the deck, as they also had to be protected against the adverse effects of salty seawater.

This was done with the aid of a cocoon of Eronal, an artificial substance developed by the firm of Dade Inc, which could be quickly applied with a spray-gun. After drying, the substance formed a resilient skin that enclosed the entire aircraft. On arrival at the destination, the cocoon could be removed without any problem. This preservation method proved itself on innumerable occasions during the Allied transportation of aircraft from the most distant theatres of war.

As soon as they arrived in the USA, the valuable freight cargoes of German spoils were taken to Newark Army Air Field and handed over to the US Materiel Command. Here, the protective cocoon was removed, the aircraft prepared and subsequently test-flown. As already mentioned, a Ju 388 was among the selected booty. The example concerned was a Ju 388L, whose life history is outlined below.

History of the Ju 388L, *Werk-Nr* 560049

The life history of *Werknummer* 560049 began at the Weserflug, more precisely at the Liegnitz works in Upper Silesia, where the aircraft was finally assembled. Various fuselage parts had been manufactured at the ATG as well as in the factory halls of the Niedersächsischen Metallwerke Brinkmann & Mergel in Hamburg-Harburg. Unfortunately, the exact time of manufacture cannot be established. This reconnaissance aircraft was a version of the Ju 388, of which 50 examples in all were completed, but which was never delivered to the Luftwaffe.

In May 1945, US troops occupied the ATG at Merseburg where, besides a number of other aircraft, 560049 was captured. This factory-fresh machine was first flown to Kassel-Waldau where it was received by the 10th Air Depot Group on 20th May 1945. During the following weeks, it was thoroughly examined: for good reason, since the intention was to ferry the aircraft over to Cherbourg, France. From there, the brand-new Ju 388 still had an extensive voyage ahead of it to the New World – sadly,

The Ju 388L (*Werknummer* 560049) in its new home in the USA which it would never leave. The original swastika insignia was reapplied by US personnel but not in conformity with standard German practice.

only a one-way ticket had been purchased for it. The beginning of this trip had been scheduled for 17th June 1945 when this aircraft, already rare for its time, began its journey to an airfield in the neighbourhood of Cherbourg. The Ju 388, although admittedly a unique example, was but one of many aircraft on the abovementioned 'passenger list'. Enclosed in a watertight covering, the 560049 was first hoisted up by a crane and then towed with the help of two trailers to the awaiting *Reaper*. Suspended on the hook of a floating gantry, the Ju 388 was then raised and, following a gentle landing onto the deck of the carrier, was then fastened down. It was July 1945 when its journey into an unknown future began. On arrival on the other side of the *Großen Teich* (Great Pond, as the Atlantic is colloquially termed in Germany), its path then led to the Army Air Force Base at Freeman Field. Here, the cap-

tured Ju 388 was thoroughly examined once more. Having been established as flightworthy, the aircraft soon completed its initial test flights for its new owner. During a press briefing in the course of which captured aircraft were displayed, some demonstration flights of the Ju 388, as well as a number of other captured aircraft, took place.

On 30th September 1945, 560049 left Freeman Field for the large US Test Centre at Wright Field for further trials. Some nine months later, in June 1946, the series of tests came to an end and the aircraft was ferried back to Freeman Field. Interest in it disappeared once its technical details had been examined and recorded in Technical Report F-TR-1138-ND in October 1946. Several other aircraft, among them the Do 335 that had been assigned to the USAAF, ended up with a scrap dealer. If only such rare exhibits could have been saved and preserved for posterity! But only a few of those in responsible positions had the foresight or the will to bring this about. However, there were certainly

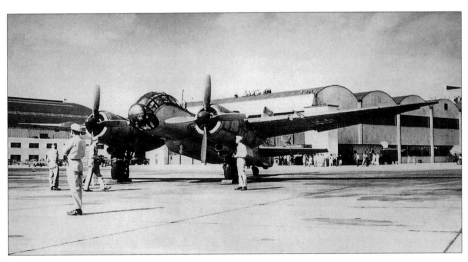

Top: **The new owner gave the aircraft a new identity: Foreign Equipment FE 4010.**

Above centre: **As the sole existing example worldwide, 560049 has been languishing for decades at Silver Hill, Maryland, as confirmed by innumerable photos on the internet.**

Above: **The same aircraft during an 'Open Day', where the American public was given an opportunity to marvel at former enemy technology.**

The Ju 388 V6 sports British insignia. Evenually scrapped, its markings PE-IF were not overpainted. In the background a Fieseler *Storch* (Stork) and a Messerschmitt Bf 108 can be seen, the latter still bearing its original insignia.

more pressing problems to worry about than preserving enemy aircraft. The USAAF as well as the US Navy were both undergoing restructuring at the time, so although regrettable, it is not surprising that priorities lay elsewhere.

'Our' Ju 388 had also been scheduled for the aircraft graveyard. Initially, it was intended to transfer it to the scrapyard at Davis Monthan, but eventually on 26th September 1946 it arrived at Park Ridge, Illinois. Fortunately, the National Air & Space Museum expressed interest in the aircraft. As had happened with other types, its provisional final journey was to the Smithsonian Institution's depository at Silver Hill, Maryland. Here, this fine specimen vegetated in highly valuable but equally neglected company for more than five decades. But at least this and a number of otherwise irreplaceable examples have been preserved for future generations rather than winding up as a frying-pan or other utensil for the American housewife.

The proverbial 'light at the end of the tunnel' comes in the form of the Dulles Center, currently under construction, in which the majority of veterans from Silver Hill will be rehoused. Prior to that, however, will come the hard work, as all of the exhibits located there will have to undergo restoration to a greater or lesser extent before making their debut in the newly built museum halls. The emphasis here is on 'greater', when one recalls, for example, the good old Do 335 which survived the years in Silver Hill in an anything but undamaged state. For the Ju 388, many an expert restorer will have to be involved in order to transform it into a worthy exhibit. Why not follow the example of the last remaining Do 335 *Ameisenbär* (Anteater)? Here, however, the interest and initiative of competent people and institutions in Germany would be required. Whether such interest actually exists is questionable. The thought of exhibiting this fascinating aircraft – on loan, at least, in its country of origin – is undoubtedly extremely inspiring for many of us.

Flight-Testing in Great Britain

In competition with the other Allies, the British also attempted to retain a large portion of the war spoils. In the territory that they occupied after the invasion, there were no fewer than 4,810 motorised aircraft and 291 gliders. Under the 'Disarming Plan', the vast majority of these were destroyed and therefore prevented from being put to any further use. In this case, too, a number of specialist teams followed immediately behind the combat troops with the aim of taking possession of high-value technology and documents, as well as the individuals responsible for them. The intention was to secure as quickly as possible a technological advantage over other nations, particularly in view of the disintegrating coalition with the East. The financial aspect was also extremely important. Huge quantities of design drawings, calculations and other material changed ownership. Patent rights were no longer worth the paper they were written on. This was also a form of reparations payment that took place with the dismantling of entire factories. Millions had been spent on technical innovations which they found in great numbers and were to be put to practical use. The Allies saved thousands of millions on research, as well as saving valuable time in terms of development of high-value weapons technology since much of the experience and expertise gained in Germany could be quickly applied with the help of numerous German technicians.

It is not therefore surprising that a collection of captured weapons underwent intensive testing in Great Britain. Besides the obligatory Me 109 and Fw 190, the 'stars' of German aircraft manufacture of the day – the Ar 234, Me 262, Do 335 and Ju 388 – were among them.

The last-mentioned aircraft was the Ju 388 L-1, *Werknummer* 500006. This machine, the Ju 388 V6, at the date of capture by US troops, was located at the E-Stelle Tarnewitz. In June 1945, British units occupied the E-Stelle. What the Germans had not already transported elsewhere, sunk in the sea, or had not already been requisitioned by the Americans, became available to the British evaluation and test centres. The captured Ju 388 L-1 (V6) was given a new identity. It was assimilated into the British experimental aircraft park as AIR MIN 83 (AM 83), the Air Ministry markings having been painted on freehand on both sides of the fuselage, with the national insignia overpainted. The Luftwaffe *Balkenkreuz* and swastikas were now obscured beneath the accurately placed British insignia. Since Tarnewitz was to have come under the Soviet occupation zone in the coming months, most of what was found to be of significance there was evacuated in June. The Ju 388 was to be ferried to Lübeck, but in order to achieve this a suitable pilot was needed. The latter was found in Hermann Gatzemeier who had been brought over to Tarnewitz at short notice from the internment camp near Grevesmühlen. For the ferry flight, neither Gatzemeier nor his aircraft mechanic was allowed to be equipped with a parachute. Flight altitude and speed had been clearly defined, and any attempt at an escape in flight would be quashed by the accompanying Spitfire. According to author Phil Butler in his book, *War Prizes*[1], the ferry flight had already taken place in May 1945, but it in fact took place in June 1945. The next leg, a ferry flight from Schleswig to Matching, occurred on 22nd August 1945, the machine finally arriving in Farnborough on 1st September 1945. Here, the Junkers formed part of the German Aircraft Exhibition which enabled the specialists to make further discoveries about German technical expertise. The aircraft remained there until April 1946 while Squadron Leader McCarty carried out flight-testing. The Ju 388's final location was in the College of Aeronautics at Cranfield in 1948. Somewhat later this aircraft also succumbed to the melting oven and only a few components of its hydraulics systems survived for demonstration purposes for quite a number of years.

The Ju 388 in the Soviet Union

As with the Allied Powers in the West, a large number of intact or slightly damaged Luftwaffe aircraft also fell into the hands of the Soviets. For example, Soviet troops found around 300(!) new Fw 190s and Me 109s on an Austrian airfield. Two fighter regiments of the Baltic Fleet were equipped with the Fw 190Ds that had been captured in East Prussia. Besides the normal Ju 52, Ju 88, He 111, Me 109 and

Me 110, the Soviets also found aircraft in the high-tech class. So the red star also adorned examples of the Ar 234, Me 163 and Me 262 as well as the He 162, and even a Do 335 was reported to have been among the captured aircraft. Unfortunately, there are no concrete details given in published aeronautical literature. Definitely confirmed, however, is the use of the Ju 388 in Soviet service. In his book, *Under the Red Star*,[2] Frederik Geust: includes a photo of regrettably very poor quality that does not enable a positive identification to be made. The sole clue is that it bears the Soviet star on the fin. During the period 1948-1951, it was used as a towcraft for the DFS 346 programme and, in all, 24 such flights with the Ju 388 were made. Later flight trials of the DFS 346 were undertaken with a Boeing B-29.[3]

Many will ask the question: How did the Russians come to get a B-29? The answer is that a few of these bombers had to make an emergency landing in Siberia following an attack on Japan and were not returned. The Tupolev Tu-4

subsequently appeared as a 'pirated copy' of the B-29. Both the Americans and British knew very well why they held back their strategic bombers from the Soviets within the terms of the Lend-Lease Agreement. The forthcoming 'Ice Age' between the soon-to-be-formed Power Blocks was already foreseeable even in wartime.

But to return to the anonymous Ju 388. In 1950 further tests followed – 12 in all were assigned to the Ju 388. A further two flights were carried out by the B-29. Author Horst Lommel in his book *Vom Höhenaufklärer zum Raumgleiter*[4] attributes towed flight trials with the Ju 388 initially to the year 1950. Prior to this, related flight trials (with the DFS 346 rescue capsule) are reported to have been conducted with a B-25 medium bomber from among the Lend-Lease aircraft.

In the book by Alexandrov and Petrov *Die deutschen Flugzeuge in russischen und sowjetischen Diensten, Band 2*,[5] a Ju 388 is portrayed in several pages of extremely interesting photographs. The aircraft, a Ju 388L-1, was undoubtedly a completely different example from that which took part in the DFS 346 programme. It is highly likely that it was the aircraft which in 1945/46 had been test-flown by Soviet

test pilots, along with the Ar 234, He 162, Me 163 and Me 262. It is not possible to assign either a *Werknummer* or call-sign markings from either Ju 388. Nor is it possible to estimate the number of Ju 388s captured by the Soviets. Readers with any relevant information on this matter are again requested to 'bring light into the darkness', as only vague references to this topic have so far been found.

Ju 488 V403 three-view drawing with capacities and locations of the eight wing and six fuselage fuel tanks.

Footnotes

1 *War Prizes*: Phil Butler; Midland Counties, 1994.
2 *Under the Red Star – Luftwaffe Aircraft in the Soviet Union*: Carl-Fredrick Geust; Airlife Publishing Ltd, 1993.
3 *Tupolev Tu-4 – Soviet Superfortress*: Yefim Gordon & Vladimir Rigmant; Midland Publishing, 2002. Provides more details of the B-29/DFS 346 flight-tests – Translator.
4 *Geheimprojeke des DFS – Vom Höhenaufklärer zum Raumgleiter (DFS Secret Projects – From the High-altitude Reconnaissance Aircraft to the Space Glider) 1935-1945*: Horst Lommel; Motorbuch Verlag, 2000.
5 *Die deutschen Flugzeuge in russischen und sowjetischen Diensten (German Aircraft in Russian and Soviet Service) 1941-1951 Vol. 2*: Andrei Alexandrov & Gennadi Petrov; Flugzeug Publications GmbH, 1998.

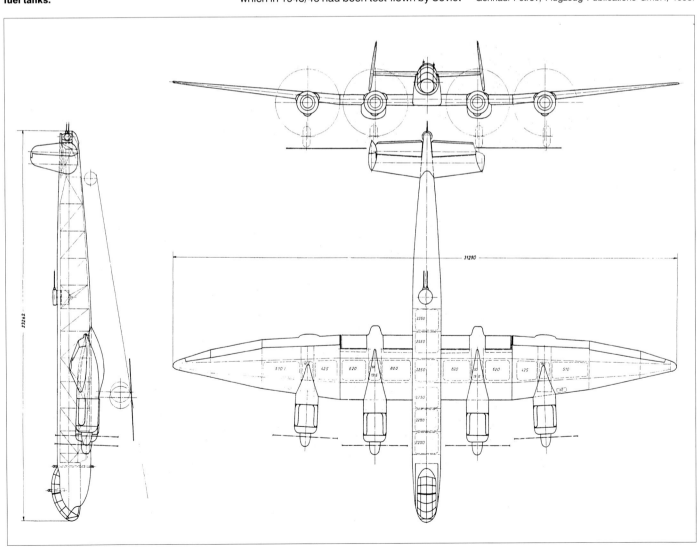

Chapter Twelve

The Ju 488

Long-range Bomber and Reconnaissance Aircraft

The 'Baukasten' Principle –
A Concept for Rapid Manufacture

The Ju 488 belonged to the Baukasten (building-block) type of manufacture, consisting of components of the Ju 88, Ju 188, Ju 288 and Ju 388. Other types had been developed in this way, one of the most well-known examples of this principle being the twin-fuselage He 111Z, used as a towcraft and planned as a twin-fuselage bomber. It comprised two He 111H fuselages joined by a new wing centre section. Several projects of this nature existed, one of the most bizarre was the similar Ju 290Z proposal, to have consisted of two Ju 290 fuselages joined by a common wing centre section. Such rare creations culminated in the Ju 390. More realistic was Messerschmitt's P.1090 Baukasten project which had roughly the dimensions of the Me 410. It was to have been employed in almost every conceivable role and therefore make an important contribution to type reduction in the Luftwaffe. Although it existed only on the drawing board, it was designed to have exchangeable groups of sub-assemblies such as the cockpit, fuselage centre section and wings, each configured to meet the requirements of the intended role. Whether this design would have proved itself in practice remains unanswered. A number of other examples from German design offices could also be cited here. This principle had also been employed on the other side of the Atlantic, where North American had developed the P-82 (later F-82) Twin-Mustang, built of two P-51H 'lightweight' Mustangs, but which did not see operational service in World War Two.

A 100% Baukasten aircraft, had been developed in the USA by the Fisher firm with its XP-75 fighter, consisting of components of the Mustang, the Chance Vought Corsair, Curtiss Warhawk and Douglas Dauntless. When manufacture ceased in October 1944, only six series-built aircraft had been completed.

Development, Manufacture
and Fate of the Ju 488 Prototypes

Returning to the German aviation industry and more specifically to Junkers. In the meantime, the development of the He 177 had been severely disrupted as a result of technical problems coupled with numerous accidents. The bomber had still not been able to display its fitness for frontline service satisfactorily. Time

was passing and the war situation was becoming ever more catastrophic for Germany. Manufacturing time was a decisive factor in bringing a new, effective weapon to the Luftwaffe. As a logical consequence it was decided to create something new out of what had already been tried and tested. The Ju 488 therefore appeared in a relatively short time at the end of 1943, constructed out of components of the Ju 388 as well as from the Ju 88, Ju 188 and Ju 288. Two different configurations were envisaged: a long-range bomber, and a long-range reconnaissance aircraft, for which Dipl.-Ing. Ernst Zindel was responsible. Since production capacity at Dessau was to a large extent overloaded due to other construction programmes, it was decided to involve Latécoère at Toulouse. The French manufacturer was assigned the task of taking over the design and construction of the fuselage and wing centre section of the Ju 488. The manufacture of the outer wing sections was carried out by Junkers in Bernburg and the tailplane was assembled in Dessau. Latécoère concentrated on construction of the first two prototypes whose fuselages took shape under the designations Ju 488 V401 and V402. Following completion, the fuselages and wing sections were to have been transported by rail to Bernburg where, according to the plan, the two prototypes would have undergone final assembly. The question then arises: Why were the outer wings not delivered to Toulouse? Presumably the precise fitting of the components had to be checked at the final assembly location.

As in the past, events did not go according to plan. Approximately one month after the Allied invasion of the Continent, the French Resistance, known as the Maquis, became active in Toulouse. During the night of 16/17th July 1944, a French sabotage unit led by M Ellissalde broke into the factory and carried out a wrecking operation using explosives, in the course of which the Ju 488 assemblies were severely damaged. The Ju 488 programme, never recovered from this severe setback.

Before this event occurred, the RLM had already decided upon the construction of four further prototypes. Designated Ju 488 V403 to V406, these underwent the necessary flight trials. Unlike the V401 and V402 powered by the BMW 801TJ, these four were to have used the more powerful Jumo 222A/B and E/F power-

plants. Owing to the rapid Allied advance, co-operation with Latécoère was no longer an option. After a few months, German firms had already been pushed back so far that the war had been brought within the borders of the Reich. In view of this, further work on a long-range bomber required a significant amount of optimism.

As a consequence, the project was leading nowhere. The four Junkers-built prototypes were to have formed the basis for the initial Ju 488A-series version, but the end came comparatively quickly. Although no sabotage unit was responsible in this case, it was traceable to the long-overdue RLM decision to put an end to such intensive programmes. With regard to the phrase 'long-overdue decision', it should be said that the Luftwaffe needed everything other than a strategic bomber that was able to take revenge on British and Soviet, and even on American, centres of population. Such operations would only have made sense with the use of atomic weapons. Research conducted by reputable historians and participating scientists, indicated these weapons were not available. In this connection, mention should be made of Friedrich Georg's book, Hitlers Siegeswaffen.* In many years of painstaking work, he took up this highly controversial topic. Georg undoubtedly carried out intensive research, and questions much that had been previously published on the subject of 'German A-Weapons'. Admittedly, these expositions often read like a work of science fiction where no tangible evidence is to be found, but it is simply not possible to provide definite proof when the archives containing the relevant documents still remain classified. If these really exist, plausible explanations might become available on some of the up-to-now incomprehensible decisions that were taken concerning the Luftwaffe.

* Friedrich Georg: Hitlers Siegeswaffen (Hitler's Victory Weapons), Vol 1, Luftwaffe und Marine, Amun-Verlag, November 2000.

With Hiroshima or Nagasaki in mind, single aircraft carrying atomic weapons could achieve the destructive effects of an armada of bombers. The operational results of a German bomber could also have been achieved had it been able to reach its target in the face of enemy air superiority. Research in this area was carried out, but could not be put to the test.

For the successful conventional employment of German large bombers, a whole fleet would have been necessary. In view of the ever-increasing limitations on all resources, such plans were completely unrealistic. In addition, such bomber formations would have required intact airfields and smooth functioning logistics for successful operations, both of which were impossible to fulfil in the deteriorating war situation. Therefore, the RLM directive to abandon the Ju 488 programme in November 1944 was correct and, with it, plans for the Ju 488A series in mid 1945 were pointless.

The development effort already expended, at least in terms of planning, would have been of use to another country, for as in various other spheres of activity, the Japanese made known their interest in the Ju 488. On 28th February 1945, the design drawings and corresponding production requirements for the Ju 488 were officially released.

The engineering of the Ju 488 is given only in very general terms in the Junkers description outlined below.

JFM Ju 488 *Baubeschreibung* (Construction Description)

The Ju 488 four-engined low-wing monoplane is a further development of the Ju 388 from which the pressurised cabin and outer wings have been adopted. Development has been aimed at creating an aircraft that enables the crew not only to perform unhindered at high altitudes but also to attain these altitudes rapidly despite the increased flying weight.

The ability to carry large loads enables the machine to achieve a high radius of action and, by reason of the powerplant arrangement, to achieve the highest possible safety. All of this predestined it as an ideal long-range reconnaissance or bomber aircraft.

Principal data are: Stress Group H, Application Group 3, Crew 3. Span: 31.29m (102ft 7⅞in), wing area 88m² (947.20ft²), take-off weight 29,000kg (63,933 lb) and maximum landing weight 25,000kg (55,115 lb).

Airframe

Fuselage: The nose crew compartment and its installations are taken from the Ju 388. The appropriate operating levers and engine control instruments are correspondingly doubled to cater for the four powerplants. Additionally, a periscope will be installed for the observer. Up to the tail end, the fuselage forms a continuous load-bearing steel tube segment. Six of its compartments contain large fuel tanks, each of the same capacity. At their extremities are the B-Stand weapon station, the dinghy and two cameras, and in subsequent compartments, the tail turret ammunition and wireless equipment console. Behind the empennage and tailwheel is the tail armament position. The forward fuel-carrying portion of the fuselage is covered with light alloy, the rear portion made of wood and covered with fabric.

Undercarriage: This consists of four individual mainwheel oleo units and a tailwheel. The outer mainwheels have a diameter and thickness of 1,220 x 445mm (48 x 17.5in), the inner mainwheels of 1,320 x 480mm (52 x 18.9in) and the tailwheel 780 x 260mm (30.7 x 10.2in) – data added by author. Outer wheel track is 14.9m (48ft 10⅝in) inner wheel track 6.5m (21ft 3⅞in).

Wing: Cantilever wing construction. The outer sections, taken from the Ju 388, are joined to a new centre section of 10.7m (33ft 1¼in) span. The wing centre section is made of dural with strengthening bands on the outer sheet skin and has a rectangular plan form, the wing increasing in thickness towards the fuselage. Between the main spars 1 and 2, there are two bays on the wing centre section upper side for the installation of two bag-type fuel tanks and a lubricant tank behind the inner engine. The wings house a total of eight fuel tanks, four are in each wing half and have a fuel quick-emptying facility. A total of 15 oxygen bottles, five for each crew member, are housed in the wing.

Empennage: The cantilever tailplane, twin fins and rudders are taken unaltered from the Ju 388.

Controls: Elevator and aileron movement takes place via the control column in the centre of the pilot's position. Rudder control is by means of adjustable rudder pedals. The trim tabs for the elevator, ailerons and rudder are operated by handwheels.

Powerplant

The 9-8222E unit is intended for installation, comprising the Jumo 222E of 2,500hp at take-off and 2,180hp climb and combat power. Rated altitude is 11,500m (37,730ft).

Airscrews: These are Jumo VS 19 four-bladed automatic variable-pitch airscrews of 4m (13ft 1½in) diameter.

Fuel System: The fuel system is made up of a total of 14 fuel tanks, eight in the wings and six in the fuselage. Those in the wing centre section are bag-tanks, the outer tanks protected and the inner unprotected. Of the similarly built tanks in the fuselage, three have no protective coverings. The innermost wing tanks and the outer wing centre section serve as fuel feed tanks. The unprotected fuselage tanks located fore, between and aft of the wing spars have a fuel quick-emptying facility.

Lubrication System: The four engines each have a separate lubricant oil tank, housed behind the engine to the rear of the transverse mounting points, plus three auxiliary oil tanks in the wings.

Equipment

Armament: Defensive armament consists of a B-Stand with a twin FBL-B 151Z in the fuselage and a tail H-Stand with a twin FHL 131Z rotatable turret.

Cameras: Installation consists of 2 x Rb 50/30.

Armour Protection: Unitary seat with back and head protection for the pilot, back armour protection for the observer, armoured panels in the rear cabin hood and armour plating of the upper portion of the rear wall of the crew compartment.

Communications Items:
- FuG 10 UHF/VHF with Peil G6
- FuG 25a IFF
- FuG 101a electrical altimeter
- FuG 16Z(Y) crew intercom
- FuG 217 warning device
- Fu Bl 2F blind-landing receiver

Safety Installations: The oxygen equipment, which formerly consisted of 12 bottles in the right wing, is increased to 15 bottles in the same area on the other wing half. Wing de-icing is by warm air from the engines. The wing centre section is not de-iced.

Further Remarks on the Ju 488

Junkers description provides only a very general overview of the technology, so it would be useful to give more detailed information here. The Ju 488 was built on the *Baukasten* principle and incorporated the following components of the Ju 88, Ju 188, Ju 288 and Ju 388:
- Forward fuselage: Pressure-sealed high-altitude pressurised cabin of the Ju 388K
- Empennage components: From the Ju 288C
- Wing: The two outer sections from the Ju 388K
- Undercarriage: All four components of the Ju 188/Ju 388. (Other sources mention the use of Ju 188E components – Author)
- Bomb bay pannier: Of wooden construction, it stemmed from the Ju 388K.

New to the design was the wing centre section as well as various fuselage groups of components made of steel tubing, aluminium, wood, and fabric sheeting. The fuselage proper up to the tail region comprised a welded steel-tube structure covered with dural up to a point just before the B-Stand. Aft of this rear main separating bulkhead, the tried and trusted but now outmoded fabric covering was used in order to economise on 'strategic materials'. In the V401 and V402 prototypes, the shape of the fuselage differed significantly from the succeeding planned prototypes. Fuselage height and width was increased over the whole length. From the V403 onwards, the deepened wooden bomb pannier was to be dispensed with.

Changes were also made to the powerplant. Whereas in the first two prototypes power was provided by the BMW 801TJ, all succeeding machines were to have had the more powerful Jumo 222A/B and E/F engines. These powerful Junkers-Jumo engines, which for a variety of reasons never attained series production, condemned from the very beginning many an otherwise highly promising project as there were no other engines of equivalent power available. The exceptions were the so-called 'double engines'. The power difference between the 1,810hp BMW 801TJ and the 2,500hp Jumo 222A/B was almost 700hp. In a four-engined aircraft, this amounted to a power difference of 2,760hp more than the BMW 801TJ.

Initial weight calculations of a mere 23 tonnes (50,706 lb) were soon superseded. Subsequent calculations initially gave a figure of 33.7 tonnes (74,295 lb) which later increased to an impressive take-off weight of 36 tonnes (79,336 lb). This weight class applied to the V403 to V406 prototypes and the Ju488A. To achieve adequate performance, powerplants of the Jumo 222 class were unavoidable. Engine power was to have been taken up by four-bladed Junkers VS19 airscrews of 4m (13ft 1½in) diameter.

The fuel capacity was divided among a total of 14 bag-tanks. In a works illustration of 9.4.1944 referring to the V403, the following quantities were listed:

- Fuselage tanks   6 x 2,250 litres = 13,500 litres
- Wing centre section 2 x 820 litres =   1,640 litres
- Wing centre section 2 x 620 litres =   1,240 litres
- Wing outer sections 2 x 425 litres =   850 litres
- Wing outer sections 2 x 510 litres =   1,020 litres

This gives an overall total of 18,450 litres of B4 fuel. Four further variants with total fuel capacities of 17,550 and 15,500 litres for the long-range reconnaissance, and 12,000 and 10,400 litres for the bomber, are included in the Technical Data table at the end of the chapter.

The lubricant oil installation in the case of the long-range reconnaissance models consisted of 700kg (1,543 lb) and 600kg (1,323 lb), and 500kg (1,102 lb) and 400kg (882 lb) for the bomber respectively. The tanks were located between the engine transverse attachment points, as well as three tanks within the wings.

The V403 drawing of 9th April 1944 shows the following lubricant quantities:
- Inner engines: 2 x 195 litres = 390 litres
- Outer engines: 2 x 105 litres = 210 litres
- Auxiliary tanks: 2 x 50 litres = 100 litres, plus
                                    1 x 40-litre tank.
The overall total is 740 litres.

The new rectangular wing centre section had a span of 10.7m (35ft 1¼in). The wing, built of dural, was a two-spar structure whose profile thickness reduced towards the wingtips. The centre section housed not only four fuel and four lubricant tanks but also the inner powerplants and the four landing flaps. As mentioned earlier, the outer wings came from the Ju388.

The massive Ju488 rested on four separate mainwheels, each retracting rearwards hydraulically to rest in the bays behind the powerplants. Each of the inner and outer undercarriage components had a single wheel of different dimensions, the inner pair measuring 1,320 x 480mm (52 x 18.9in), supporting a load of 9 tonnes (19,841 lb). Wheels of this size were also featured in the Fw191, He 343, Hs130, Ju90, Ju290 and Ju353. The outer units each had wheels of 1,220 x 445mm (48 x 17.5in). Permissible load here was 7.5 tonnes (16,534 lb). Wheels of these dimensions were also used in the He177 and He343. The tailwheel, was 780 x 260mm (30.7 x 10.2in), and able to support loads up to 3.1 tonnes (6,834 lb) and was used in the Fw191 and He177. Track of the inner wheels was 6.5m (21ft 3⅞in) and that of the outer wheels was 14.9m (48ft 10⅝in).

Details on the Ju488 variants powered by the Jumo 222A/B and E/F will be found in the data table.

Too Late! – Ju 488 Production

As the Ju488 was a so-called *Baukasten* aircraft, it would have been theoretically capable – assuming sufficient resources and production capacities – of being rapidly built in large numbers. However, it is questionable whether it would have been sensible to put this aircraft into production, since Heinkel was working on the He177 and He277. Other manufacturers, such as Messerschmitt with the Me264, Focke-Wulf with the Ta400, or even Junkers itself with the large Ju290 and Ju390 or the giant EF100, offered a wide range of equally large aircraft, not to mention many other projects that were non-starters for one reason or another. The twin-fuselage Ju290 already referred to, out of which the Ju390 appeared in modified form, count among the classic examples where such madness was allowed to go unchecked.

As stated earlier, the two Ju488 V401 and V402 prototypes were already under construction in France. A further four prototypes were scheduled to follow. Because of the gaps in documentary sources available at the present time, nothing definite is known concerning further production plans and numbers, but undoubtedly such plans had already been made. The directive to terminate the programme finally came in November 1944.

All production plans, to whatever extent these may have called for production of the Ju488A-series from mid- 1945, were superfluous as a result of the capitulation in May 1945.

Soap Bubbles –
Japan as Licence Manufacturer

One way for German aircraft firms to bring about manufacture of their aircraft, albeit with few credits, was to offer manufacturing licences or just know-how to foreign firms. To convert licences into jingling coins was, and is, nothing unusual even in wartime, when logically negotiations took place only with friendly, allied or neutral countries. Junkers even settled its payments due on licence fees to Hamilton-Standard (for the Junkers-Hamilton propellers) whilst at war with the USA in 1943, through Lloyd Aero Boliviano.

From 1942 onwards, the German aviation industry increasingly sought to sell licences for its products to its allies or at least to neutrals abroad, such as Italy, Bulgaria, Romania and Hungary. Other so-called neutral states which undertook regular trade with the warring factions on both sides were Turkey, Sweden, Spain and Switzerland. Interest, however, centred on Japan. As the war progressed, Japanese delegations 'opened the door' to German manufacturers. The Japanese firm of Kawasaki showed great interest with a project worth 30 million Reichsmarks to support the construction of a large-scale production centre. Added to that came licence rights for RM 9 million to build the Ju488. The Japanese also expressed an interest in the Jumo 213, worth RM 4.32 million. In addition, licensing rights were granted to Japan for other products of the Junkers-Werke, including the Jumo 004 turbojet and the piston-engined Jumo 222 and Jumo 223, and aircraft manufacturing rights were requested for the Ju288, Ju388, Ju488 and the Ju390. A total figure of RM 130 million was involved. Drawings and plans in relation to manufacturing methods, constructional components or complete powerplants were to be transported by submarine on the long voyage to Japan, but during the period from 1943 to 1945 this was far from being a straightforward undertaking. Several attempts foundered as a result of the vigilance of Allied warships and aircraft crews, and only a very small proportion of the data wanted by the Japanese actually reached them. This fact affected not only Junkers but also Messerschmitt, Henschel, Heinkel and Dornier.

The Trade Agreement of 20th January 1943 was really no more than symbolic, since regular long-distance communication via submarine, blockade runners or air was considerably hindered by the increasing Allied air superiority in all theatres of the war. On 2nd March 1944, a further agreement between the two remaining Axis Powers was ratified that was once more to provide German expertise to the Japanese war economy. For various reasons, Japan was able to profit from this in only a very small way. The die had already been cast for Japan; defeat was inevitable and it was only a matter of time.

Ju 488 Technical Data

	Ju 488 Long-range Reconnaissance	Ju 488 Long-range Bomber	Ju 488 Long-range Reconnaissance	Ju 488 Long-range Bomber
Powerplants				
Designation	Jumo 222A/B(-3)	Jumo 222A/B(-3)	Jumo 222E/F(-1)	Jumo 222 E/F(-1)
Take-off power (x 4)*	2,500hp + 130kg	2,500hp + 130kg	2,500hp + 130kg	2,500hp + 130kg
Climb and combat power				
at sea level	2,200hp + 112kg	2,200hp + 112kg	2,180hp + 102kg	2,180hp + 180kg
at 7,200m (23,620ft)	1,910hp + 162kg	1,910hp + 162kg	1,650hp + 180kg	1,650hp + 180kg
Dimensions				
Wingspan	31.29m (102' 7⅞")	31.29m (102' 7⅞")	31.29m (102' 7⅞")	31.29m (102' 7⅞")
Overall length	23.24m (76' 3")	23.24m (76' 3")	23.24m (76' 3")	23.24m (76' 3")
Height	7.10m (23' 3½")	7.10m (23' 3½")	7.10m (23' 3½")	7.10m (23' 3½")
Wing area, m² (ft²)	88 (947.2)	88 (947.2)	88 (947.2)	88 (947.2)
Aspect ratio	11.126	11.126	11.126	11.126
Fuel capacities (24.7.1944)†				
Fuselage tanks, litres	12,800	7,250	10,750	5,650
Wing tanks, litres	4,750	4,750	4,750	4,750
Total capacity, litres	17,550	12,000	15,500	10,400
Weights				
Equipped weight, kg (lb)	21,200 (46,738)	21,000 (46,297)	21,000 (46,297)	21,000 (46,297)
Fuel weight, kg (lb)	13,500 (29,762)	8,900 (19,621)	1l,500 (25,353)	7,700 (16,975)
Lubricant weight, kg (lb)	700 (1,543)	500 (1,102)	600 (1,323)	400 (882)
Crew of three, kg (lb)	300 (661)	300 (661)	300 (661)	300 (661)
Ammunition, kg (lb)	220 (485)	220 (485)	220 (485)	220 (485)
Bombload, kg (lb)	none	5,000 (11,023)	none	5,000 (11,023)
Take-off weight, kg (lb)	36,000 (79,366)	36,000 (79,366)	33,700 (74,295)	33,700 (74,295)
Take-off wing loading, kg/m² (lbft²)	409 (83.8)	409 (83.8)	383 (78.4)	383 (78.4)
Mean flying weight, kg (lb)	29,250 (64,485)	26,550 (58,532)	27,950 (61,619)	5,850 (63,603)
Performance:				
Max speed at S/L, km/h (mph)	541 (336)	544 (338)	529 (329)	531 (330)
at 7,000m (22,965ft)	684 (425)	690 (429)	-	-
Climb rate at take-off, m/sec (ft/min)	9.2 (1,811)	9.2 (1,811)	8.85 (1742)	8.85 (1742)
Time to 6,000m (19,685ft), min	13	13	-	-
to 8,000m (26,250ft)	-	-	31.8	31.8
Range at 6,000m (19,685ft)	5,100km (3,169 miles) [1]	3,400km (2,113 miles) [3]	4,970km (3,088 miles) [5]	3,220km (2,00l miles) [7]
Range at 6,000m (19,685ft)	6,820km (4,238 miles) [2]	4,360km (2,709 miles) [4]	5,580km (3,467 miles) [6]	3,600km (2,237 miles) [8]
Service ceiling, m (ft)				
four motors	10,750 (35,270)	11,350 (37,240)	13,150 (13,150)	13,650 (13,650)
three motors	9,200 (30,185)	9,850 (32,315)	11,650 (38,220)	12,100 (39,700)
two motors	5,900 (19,355)	7,400 (24,280)	5,100 (16,740)	7,100 (23,300)
Endurance, hours	-	5.7	-	4.7
Take-off run on grass, m (ft)	1,100 (3,609)	1,060 (3,478)	1,000 (3,281)	1,000 (3,281)
to 15m (49ft)	1,420 (4,659)	1,380 (4,528)	1,310 (4,298)	1,310 (4,298)
Take-off run on concrete, m (ft)	840 (2,756)	820 (2,690)	550 (1,804)	550 (1,804)
to 15m (49ft)	1,160 (3,806)	1,140 (3,740)	870 (2,854)	870 (2,854)
Armament				
B-Stand	FDL 151Z	FDL 151Z	FDL 151Z	FDL 151Z
H-Stand	FHL 131Z	FHL 131Z	FHL 131Z	FHL 131Z
Cameras	2 x Rb 50/30	-	2 x Rb 50/30	-

* Exhaust-gas thrust in kg: 130kg (287 lb), 112kg (247 lb) and 102kg (225 lb); † According to the plan of 9.9.1944 (Ju 488 V403) the following fuel quantities were quoted: Fuselage tanks (6 x 2,250 litres), outer wing tanks (2 x 510 litres) and (2 x 425 litres), centre wing tanks (2 x 620 litres) and (2 x 820 litres), giving a total of 18,250 litres.

[1] Cruising speed (maximum): 610km/h at 6,000m (379mph at 19,685ft)
[2] Cruising speed (throttled): 480km/h at 6,000m (298mph at 19,685ft)
[3] Cruising speed (maximum): 597/622km/h at 6,000m (371/387mph at 19,685ft)
[4] Cruising speed (throttled): 487/486km/h at 6,000m (303/302mph at 19,685ft)
[5] Cruising speed (maximum): 641/672km/h at 10,000m (398/418mph at 32,810ft)
[6] Cruising speed (throttled): 551/564km/h at 10,000m (342/350mph at 32,810ft)
[7] Cruising speed (maximum): 636/678km/h at 10,000m (395/421mph at 32,810ft)
[8] Cruising speed (throttled): 556/576km/h at 10,000m (345/358mph at 32,810ft)

Translator's Note: According to an Air Min Report, data for the Ju 488 V401 and V402 were: Powerplants: 2 x BMW 801TJ of 1,810hp at take-off, wingspan 101.5ft (30.95m), length 66.7ft (20.33m), wing area 940ft² (87.33m²), aspect ratio 11.0, fuel capacity 900 gals (4,100 litres) normal, and 1,250 gals (5,700 litres) max. With a 2,000kg (4,409 lb) internal bombload, take-off weight was 50,900 lb (c.23.14 tonnes). Estimated max speed was 285mph (460km/h) at sea level, 428mph at 42,600ft (689km/h) at 13km and 385mph (620km/h) at max continuous cruising power at that altitude. Range at economical cruise was 1,280 miles (2,060km) and 1,120 miles (1,800km) at max continuous cruise, and service ceiling was 48,000ft (14,630m).

Chapter Thirteen

Small But Fine

The Aircraft in Scale

Compared to aircraft such as the Me 109, Fw 190 and He 111, the modeller has a relatively limited selection of kits available. Below, Ralf Schlüter describes his experiences with the kits from Huma, Kora and Special Hobby.

Numerous photographs and drawings are included, which reveal several details of interest to the modeller.

The Ju 288 in 1/72nd Scale

The modelling community is very poorly catered for with regard to the Ju 288. In the 1970s, a vacuum kit of the **Ju 288 V3** appeared, but it was only in 2001 that the German Huma firm produced a kit for the **Ju 288C (V103)**. These were, and still are, the entire range of models available.

Let's start with the vacu-kit from Air Modell. Apart from the fact that a vacu-kit is just that, where everything except for the fuselage halves, wings, empennage surfaces and cockpit has to be self-made, it has to be said that this kit forms only a broad basis for the Ju 288 V3. The basic dimensions conform to the wingspan and length of the Ju 288 V1 and V2 prototypes. Photographs of the V3 show a larger span as well as an almost straight wing leading edge, so that extension segments have to be added to the wing structure. When doing this, the ailerons and landing flaps have to be cut out and formed separately in order to refine the poor execution of all the sheet-metal surfaces and the flaps. After completion and assembly of these sheet surfaces, trim off and/or spray along the adhesive tape. The wings should be given a new centre section so as to be an accurate fit to the fuselage, as the wing root ribs on the fuselage are positioned much too low down. Between the wing trailing edge and the tailplane leading edge, the fuselage is 8mm too short so needs to be lengthened. This becomes much easier when a new straight-sided fuselage element is attached to the cross-section of the fuselage. If you open the long bomb bay the task is made simpler as the fuselage can then be constructed from the inside as well. The long, straight bomb bay floor then provides a stable backbone for the entire fuselage. The fuselage forward component is that of the slim Ju 288A for the crew of three, and is so configured from the fuselage width and cabin layout. The internal details which have to be created from scratch should

be made with the aid of drawings and photographs, since the construction guidelines provided are incorrect. With the undercarriage, too, the modeller has to rely on photographs and good illustrations. The kit instructions are accurate only in respect of the height measurement of the individual elements of the undercarriage. The cabin is unfortunately outlined only very roughly, so that for an authentic result, a self-made mould and cabin are necessary. As with early German bombers, the surface coating for the insides is the usual RLM 02, with RLM 66 black-grey in the crew visibility range. The outer coating is the customary RLM 70/71/65 which, during the early period, carried the civil registration letters with the red/white/black national emblem on the fin and rudder. The later applied military codes were on either side of the *Balkenkreuz (*Luftwaffe cross). A fuselage band of unidentified colour completed the military finish.

The Ju 288 V103 from Huma is much more 'user-friendly' to build and, with the exception of the cockpit internal fittings, forms a solid basis for a simple assembly with good results. The impatient modeller can also use the cockpit internal parts of the Huma kit and so put together the entire aircraft from the kit box. Since Huma has been able to manufacture a superb cockpit with striking transparencies, it would be a great pity if the 'innards' of such an exotic aircraft were not correspondingly made to match. If only Huma provided a support to open the bomb bay doors, as the firm also furnishes the bomb bay flooring and the fore and aft enclosing frames as well as two SC 1000 bombs. A deeper trench on the inside of the fuselage along the edge of the door would be very helpful since the fuselage plastic material in this location is very thick. Unfortunately, Huma's adhesive transfers are also a little thick and have a tendency to cast shadows on clear varnish. As with the Ju 288 V3, it is recommended that the code letters be applied with the aid of stencils and the spray pistol. In summary, it can be said that Huma has come up with a very fine model of this exotic aircraft, which also leaves some room for personal initiative.

Opposite page:
Close-up details of the Ju 388 V3 (D-ACTF).

The Ju 388 in 1/72nd Scale

The range of kits offered in respect of this aircraft is considerably greater. Firstly, there is a vacuum conversion kit that allows one, on the basis of the Ju 188 modelling kit from Matchbox, to build all variants of the Ju 388's predecessors (the Ju 188S and Ju 188T) as well as the Ju 388 itself. For this purpose, the conversion set contains a fuselage with the FDL 131 tail armament, a fuselage nose for the Ju 388K/L, all the variants of the ventral fuselage weapon pod or pannier, as well as a set of extremely fine cockpit transparencies for the Ju 388J/K/L. Also provided are engine auxiliaries for the BMW 801TJ. Since the latter unfortunately have to be attached to the Matchbox engine annular intake ring, although of the correct length, the result is a little too narrow in terms of engine diameter. In the absence of other options, this conversion set offers a solid basis for a Ju 388-Series aircraft.

In view of newer kits for the Ju 388, however, it should only be used for building the Ju 188S and T models. As a bonus, a *Morgenstern* nose for a Ju 88G is also provided. Besides this vacuum conversion kit, there is a Ju 388K resin model manufactured by Kora, as well as the pressure die-cast kit for the Ju 388J and Ju 388K/L from the Special Hobby firm.

The kit from Kora consists of a model whose most important components are of resin, namely two one-piece wings, fuselage halves, empennage, undercarriage nacelles, propellers, wheels and powerplants. The small parts for detail finish are photo-engraved. White-metal undercarriage and an acetate cockpit hood complete the model. All parts are very cleanly finished, exterior shape and panel lines being very exact, in accordance with available drawings. On the whole, all parts give the impression that a very neat result can be obtained. The undercarriage oleo legs, however, are too plump, and I would replace them with self-made units. The accompanying decals allow completion of the Ju 388K, *Werknummer* 340405, one of the bombers found parked in Dessau that did not see service use.

The two kits from Special Hobby are based on very well manufactured pressure die-cast parts for the airframe and the engines. Undercarriage housings, cockpit fittings, engine appearance and small parts are of resin, with further small items enclosed as photo-engraved parts. Assembly is much simpler than the vacuum kit, since most parts have been made to fit exactly. In attaching the resin-made parts (cockpit and undercarriage housings) as much extraneous material as possible has to be filed off in order to insert them correctly. The seats for all three crew members are identical, which is not strictly authentic. The starboard seat does not fit into the cockpit, so right from the beginning one ought to put together the appropriate folding seat and then insert it. For several versions of the aircraft, there are very clear acetate cockpits included which when cut out accurately fit perfectly onto the appropriate model. The die-cast radar antenna array included in the kit can be very neatly attached to the model. After applying a rather thicker layer of colour, the somewhat 'flat' appearance can be improved on for what in reality were round antenna masts, giving an acceptable end result. Far better here, of course, is an exact 'scratch-build' out of hollow tubing of varying diameters which, inserted into each other, make a much better impression. Special Hobby offers two variants, the second Ju 388J variant being of 'academic' interest. It portrays the difference between the initial experimental state of the prototypes and a later construction stage. Important differences are small side windows in the lower cockpit area, the absence of the special airspeed probe and the antennas of the rearward radar warning device on the vertical fin and rudder. Colours and markings are identical.

The Ju 388K/L kit offers two variants, allowing either the reconnaissance version with the camera windows in the underfuselage pannier or the bomber without these to be built. The surface colours here are different. The reconnaissance variant, as with the Ju 388J, has the standard RLM 70/71/65, whereas the bomber has RLM 83/76 colours. It is clearly evident that the Ju 388J and Ju 388K were in fact conversions of existing Ju 188 airframes. The decals from Special Hobby in this case deserve special commendation. They are very thin, can be affixed to every skin surface detail and do not cast shadows. The impress is accurate and precise, so that the services of the manufacturer of these decals should be employed in future for all kits. If the two Special Hobby kits are built with a degree of devotion and skill they can turn out to be real 'gems'.

Lack of a Ju 488 kit

Unfortunately, any search for a model of the Ju 488 will be in vain. Only the old tried and tested 'scratch method', using various kits from suitable Junkers aircraft, a rummage in the box of spares and lots of patience will be of help here!

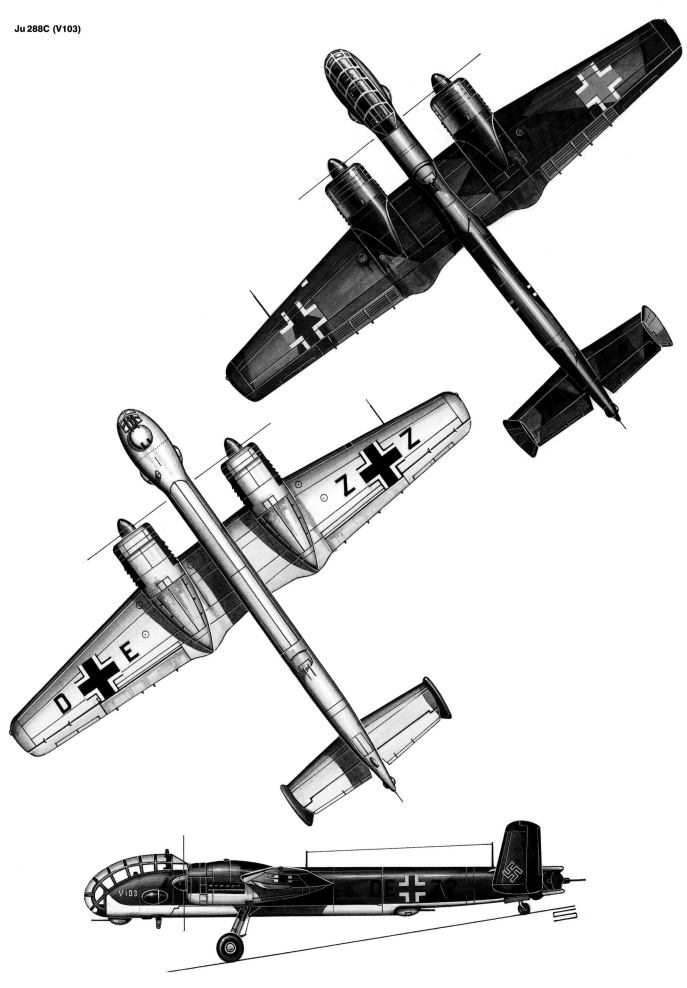

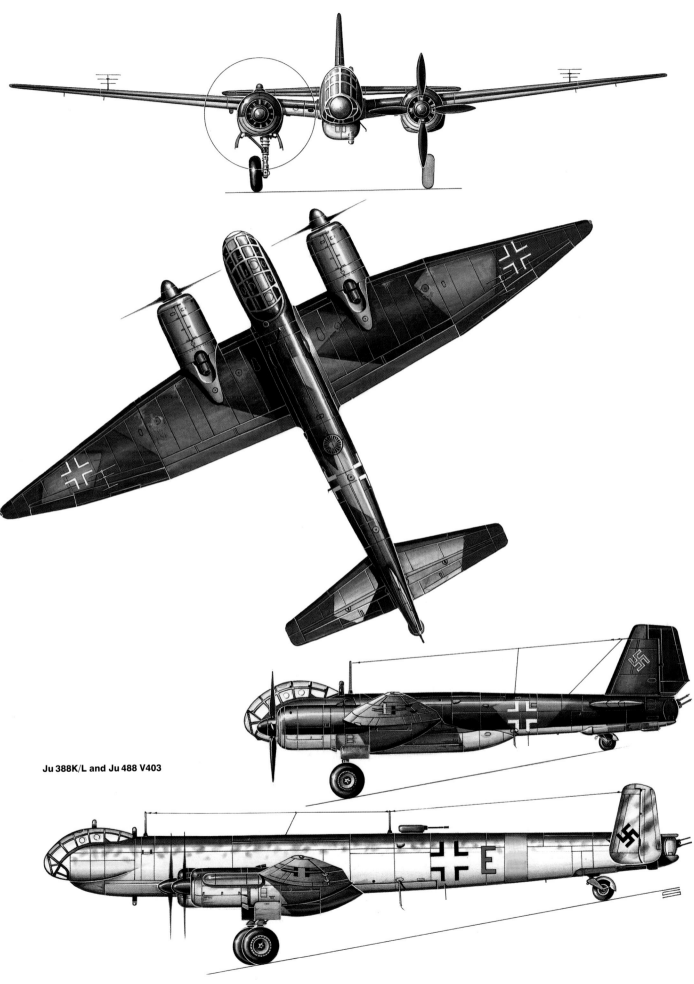

Ju 388K/L and Ju 488 V403

Above, top left and right: **Ju 288 V3 (D-ACTF) motor, side and upper views.**

Below: **Ju 288 V103 (DE+ZZ) from various perspectives.**

Above (and overleaf top): **Ju 388L, J, and K from various perspectives.**

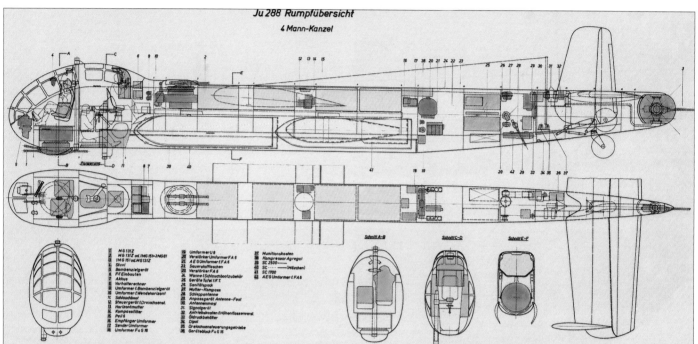

Ju 288 Rumpfübersicht
4 Mann-Kanzel

Schnitt A-B Schnitt C-D Schnitt E-F

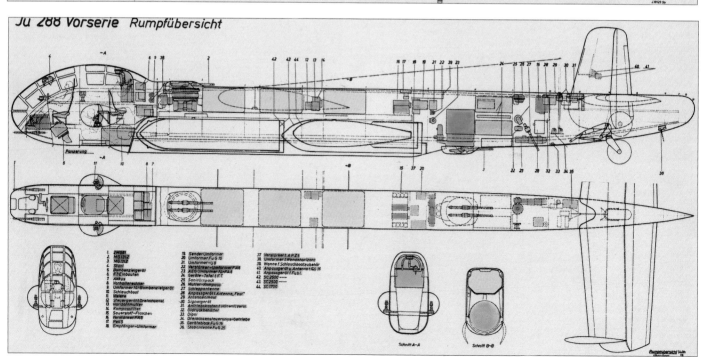

Ju 288 Vorserie Rumpfübersicht

Schnitt A-A Schnitt B-B

Two views showing the internal details of the three-crew Ju 288 V6 (upper), and the four-crew Ju 288 (lower) with numbered components.

Sources and Acknowledgements

This book has been put together based mainly on original documents, enabling a far more authentic account than is possible with secondary literature. The latter, however, has also been consulted, and comprises extracts from the following reliable published works:

Die deutsche Luftwaffe series: Bernard & Graefe Verlag
Vol 1: *Kurt Tank – Konstrukteur und Testpilot bei Focke-Wulf;* Wolfgang Wagner, 1980.
Vol 2: *Flugmotoren und Strahltriebwerke;* Gersdorff/Grasmann/Schubert, 1981.
Vol 9: *Typenhandbuch der deutschen Luftfahrttechnik;* Bruno Lange, 1986.
Vol 24: *Hugo Junkers – Pionier der Luftfahrt;* Wolfgang Wagner, 1996.

Flugzeugindustrie und Luftrüstung in Deutschland 1918-45: Lutz Budraß; Droste Verlag, Düsseldorf, 1998.

Flugzeugbewaffnung: Hanfried Schliephake; Motorbuch Verlag, Stuttgart, 1977.

Flugzeugfahrwerke: Günther Sengfelder; Motorbuch Verlag, Stuttgart, 1979.

Mighty Eighth War Diary: Roger A Freeman; Janes, London, 1981.

War Prizes: P Butler; Midland Counties, Leicester, 1994.

The author wishes to express his heartfelt thanks to all those individuals and institutions without whose kind assistance this publication would not have been possible. The majority of the photographs and documents come from the archives of the EADS Heritage, the author's collection and those of the various contributors mentioned individually below, as well as that of the publisher.

Thanks are expressed especially to Michael Baumann, Arnd Siemon and Harald Schuller, and also to Ralf Swoboda who is responsible for the informative colour illustrations. Thanks also go to Ralf Schlüter who made the attractive models of the Ju 288 and Ju 388 and who compiled the corresponding modelling report.

Written historical material has been reproduced from original aircraft handbooks or other historical records. A transcript of these documents was unavoidable as these proved unsuitable for reproduction.

Karl-Heinz Regnat

JAGDWAFFE SERIES VOLUME ONE

Volume 1, Section 1
Birth of Luftwaffe Fighter Force
Softback , 303 x 226 mm, 96 pages
c250 photos. 0 952686 75 9 **£12.95**

Volume 1, Section 2
The Spanish Civil War
Softback , 303 x 226 mm, 96 pages
c250 photos. 0 952686 76 7 **£12.95**

Volume 1, Section 3
Blitzkrieg & Sitzkrieg 1939-40
Softback , 303 x 226 mm, 96 pages
c250 photos. 0 952686 77 5 **£12.95**

Volume 1, Section 4
Attack in the West 1940
Softback, 303 x 226 mm, 96 pages
c250 photos. 0 952686 78 3 **£12.95**

JAGDWAFFE SERIES VOLUME TWO

Volume 2, Section 1
BoB Phase 1: June-July 1940
Softback, 303 x 226 mm, 96 pages
c250 photos. 1 903223 05 9 **£14.95**

Volume 2, Section 2
BoB Phase 2: Aug-Sept 1940
Softback, 303 x 226 mm, 96 pages
c250 photos. 1 903223 06 7 **£14.95**

Volume 2, Section 3
BoB Phase 3: Sept-Oct 1940
Softback, 303 x 226 mm, 96 pages
c250 photos. 1 903223 07 5 **£14.95**

Volume 2, Section 4
BoB Phase 4: Oct-Dec 1940
Softback, 303 x 226 mm, 96 pages
c250 photos. 1 903223 08 3 **£14.95**

JAGDWAFFE SERIES VOLUME THREE

Volume 3, Section 1
Strike in the Balkans: April-May 1941
Softback , 303 x 226 mm, 96 pages
c250 photos. 1 903223 20 2 **£14.95**

Volume 3, Section 2
Barbarossa: Invasion of Russia April-
May 1941. Sbk, 303 x 226 mm, 96pp
c250 photos. 1 903223 21 0 **£14.95**

Volume 3, Section 3
War over the Desert: N Africa June 1940
to June 1942. Sbk, 303 x 226 mm, 96pp,
c250 photos. 1 903223 22 9 **£14.95**

Volume 3, Section 4
The War in Russia: Jan-Oct 1942
Softback, 303 x 226 mm, 96 pages
c250 photos. 1 903223 16 4 **£14.95**

JAGDWAFFE SERIES VOLUME FOUR

Volume 4, Section 1
Holding the West: 1941 to 1943

Operations on the Western Front while a
large number of Luftwaffe units were
elsewhere on 'Barbarossa' are covered.

Softback , 303 x 226 mm, 96 pages,
17 col, 229 b/w photos, 27 col artworks
1 903223 34 2 **£14.95**

Volume 4, Section 2
The Mediterranean: 1942 to 1943

Operations over North Africa in general,
and Tunisia in particular are covered.

Softback , 303 x 226 mm, 96 pages,
8 col, 225 b/w photos, 24 col artworks
1 903223 34 2 **£14.95**

Black Cross Volume 1
JUNKERS Ju 188

Helmut Erfurth

The Ju 188 was among the most well-
known combat aircraft of World War
Two from the Junkers Flugzeug- und
Motorenwerke in Dessau. Developed
from 1941 out of the Ju 88B-series
model as an interim solution for the
Ju 288, the Ju 188 incorporated the
sum of all the military and tactical
experiences of frontline pilots together
with the technological design
possibilities in aircraft constructionand
armament at that time in Germany.

Softback, 280 x 215mm, 64 pages
30 b/w photos, 6pp of col, plus dwgs
1 85780 172 5 **£8.99**

MESSERSCHMITT Me 163
VOLUME TWO

S Ransom & Hans-Hermann Cammann

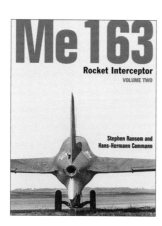

Following years of detailed research,
this is the second volume in a two
volume study of the Luftwaffe's
legendary Messerschmitt Me 163
rocket-powered interceptor.
   The authors have found incredible
new documentary material and
previously unpublished photographs,
receiving co-operation from many
former pilots who flew this radical and
daunting aircraft, as well as Allied pilots
who encountered it in combat.

Hardback, 303 x 226 mm, 224 pages,
c300 photos, 20 colour artworks
1 903223 13 X **£35.00**

ON SPECIAL MISSIONS
The Luftwaffe's Research and
Experimental Squadrons 1923-1945

J R Smith, E Creek and P Petrick

The story of the Verschuchsverband,
the Trials and Research Unit of the
Luftwaffe High Command, one of the
most intriguing, clandestine and rarely-
covered elements of the Luftwaffe
before and during World War Two.
   Using unpublished recollections
from pilots who flew secret, long-range
recce and spy-dropping missions, as
well as hundreds of rare and fascinating
photos, the book recounts the history,
operations and aircraft of the unit.

Hardback, 303 x 226 mm, 128 pages,
c360 b/w photos, 15 colour artworks
1 903223 33 4 **£19.95**

HELICOPTERS
OF THE THIRD REICH

S Coates with J C Carbonel

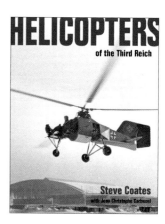

By the end of the Second World War,
the Germans were, despite minimal
funding and bitter inter-service rivalries,
technologically ahead of their American
counterparts in the development of
rotating-wing aircraft. This book is the
first comprehensive account of the
development of auto-gyros and
helicopters in Germany during 1930 to
1945 and sheds light on an unjustly
neglected area of considerable
aeronautical achievement.

Hardback, 303 x 226 mm, 224 pages,
470 b/w and colour photos, plus dwgs
1 903223 24 5 **£35.00**